SHAPING FUTURES

Shaping Futures
Learning for Competence and Citizenship

KAREN M. EVANS

LONDON AND NEW YORK

First published 1998 by Ashgate Publishing

Reissued 2018 by Routledge
2 Park Square, Milton Park, Abingdon, Oxon, OX14 4RN
711 Third Avenue, New York, NY 10017, USA

Routledge is an imprint of the Taylor & Francis Group, an informa business

Copyright © Karen M. Evans 1998

All rights reserved. No part of this book may be reprinted or reproduced or utilised in any form or by any electronic, mechanical, or other means, now known or hereafter invented, including photocopying and recording, or in any information storage or retrieval system, without permission in writing from the publishers.

Notice:
Product or corporate names may be trademarks or registered trademarks, and are used only for identification and explanation without intent to infringe.

Publisher's Note
The publisher has gone to great lengths to ensure the quality of this reprint but points out that some imperfections in the original copies may be apparent.

Disclaimer
The publisher has made every effort to trace copyright holders and welcomes correspondence from those they have been unable to contact.

A Library of Congress record exists under LC control number: 98071461

ISBN 13: 978-1-138-35211-7 (hbk)
ISBN 13: 978-1-138-35212-4 (pbk)
ISBN 13: 978-0-429-43488-4 (ebk)

Contents

Figures vi

Acknowledgements vii

Preface viii

Introduction 1

1 Education, work and citizenship: beyond the work-related curriculum 5

2 Effective workers, good citizens? Legacies of the past 25

3 Gaining the competitive edge? 43

4 Opportunity structures and status passages: metaphors for transitions to adult life 59

5 Winners and losers in transition 79

6 Competence and citizenship: which versions are required for times of critical social change? 105

7 Back to the future: from transferable skills to educated attributes 121

Bibliography 137

Figures

Figure 3.1	Full-time participation by course at 16: percentage of cohort increasing to over 70 percent by mid-90s	44
Figure 3.2	The triple track model of post-16 qualifications, NCVQ	45
Figure 3.3	Foundation 3 Target - Progress at 1996	47
Figure 3.4	Perceptions of individual responsibility for social wellbeing and career advancement	49
Figure 3.5	Full-time participation in Further Education or equivalent at 16, 17 and 18	50
Figure 3.6	General work skills: 16-20 year olds in England and Germany	52
Figure 3.7	Work commitment: 16-20 year olds in England and Germany	53
Figure 3.8	Political interest: 16-20 year olds in England and Germany	55
Figure 3.9	Employment confidence: 16-20 year olds in England and Germany	55
Figure 3.10	Employment expectations: 16-20 year olds in England and Germany	56
Figure 3.11	Inequality Trend: Changes in GINI co-efficient	57
Figure 4.1	Theoretical perspectives on transitions	74
Figure 5.1	Transition behaviour and career patterns	102
Figure 6.1	Percentages living away from home, by age	111
Figure 6.2	Modes of power interventions and outcomes	118
Figure 6.3	Variables influencing transition behaviours and outcomes	119
Figure 7.1	Education for citizenship	134

Acknowledgements

Many people have made valuable contributions to the ideas which are developed in this book. I am especially grateful to my colleagues and co-researchers in the 16-19 Initiative and the Anglo-German projects who have contributed to the perspectives and examples used, particularly John Bynner, Ken Roberts, Walter Heinz, Alan Brown and Martina Behrens.

I would also like to express thanks to my research students, Peter Rudd and Judith Jenner whose original work on aspects of youth transition has illuminated and stimulated parts of the analysis and provided additional cases and examples. I am indebted to Pam Gellatly for word-processing the manuscript and to Peter Evans and my colleague Bob Brownhill for their valuable advice on the various drafts and the final product.

Karen Evans

Preface

'I believe that citizenship, like anything else, has to be learned. Young people do not become good citizens by accident any more than they become good nurses or good engineers or good bus drivers or computer scientists. My concern is whether we offer enough encouragement to our young people to learn how to be good citizens.'

The Right Honorable Bernard Weatherill,
Commission on Citizenship, 1990

Introduction

Competence and citizenship are central themes in the life and work transitions of young adults. Competence has assumed a prominent place in discourses about the post-compulsory education and training curriculum in Britain, particularly with the introduction of National Vocational Qualifications (NVQs). Citizenship has re-entered educational debates with a new force, as concepts of 'active citizenship' have been introduced into government policy to offset criticisms of individualistic and greed driven values, in a way which emphasises voluntarism and private contribution.

Both concepts take on new dimensions when considered in the context of the changing structures of opportunity and perceived risk faced by young adults. Both practitioners and policy-makers need more holistic analyses of social dynamics against which to assess programmes and policy options, moving beyond policy-driven preoccupations with the labour market towards policy-relevant, future-oriented analysis which addresses changes in the social situation of young adults.

While the concepts of competence and of citizenship are usefully employed in discussing the processes involved in achieving adult status, both are value-laden and contested, both are socially constructed and both are employed to support particular ideological positions.

The concept of citizenship potentially provides a way of understanding the life and work transitions of early adulthood. Becoming a citizen can be seen as more than a simple matter of acquiring civil status with accompanying rights and obligations. Citizenship is being rethought as a process through which young adults exercise responsibility and social contribution while having entitlements to support and provisions which enable them to manage their own transitions to adulthood and pursue their own projects. This requires and embraces competence. This approach to citizenship requires us to consider institutional structures which constrain or enable the acquisition and recognition of the various forms of knowledge and competence which are necessary to independent existence and social contribution. The approach takes account of the part played by psycho-social processes and agency, particularly self-efficacy, or belief in one's competence and ability to act. In spanning the public and private domains of existence, it enables us to address questions of inequality and of status inconsistency at various stages of the life course.

Independence is central to notions of citizenship. This creates ambiguities for a range of social groups, including women dependent on partners as well as for young adults. In early adulthood, independence occurs incrementally and unevenly on a number of fronts. Step by step young people achieve independence from parents, not only financially but also by establishing values and beliefs of their own, making their own choices (albeit structurally constrained) and eventually by the physical separation of leaving home, either permanently or for extended periods.

This growing independence goes hand in hand with the process of establishing separate identities and with development of beliefs about their own competence as functioning and active members of society. These changes are, increasingly, provisional and reversible. Similarly, competence may be understood as necessary for achievement of economic independence and increasing time is devoted to its development, whether in its broader or narrower forms, as young adults spend extended periods in trainee or student status. Self-efficacy, or belief in one's ability to act, is also central to effective participation in social and economic structures of society. Citizenship thus potentially embraces notions of individual competence, as well as collective responsibility and contribution.

The discussion of education for competence and citizenship which follows is in seven chapters. The first chapter outlines some meanings and traditions associated with the contested concepts of citizenship and competence and argues that both concepts have 'minimal' and 'maximal' versions. Educators need to be clear about which versions to adopt, and ensure that the versions chosen are complementary, not contradictory. Chapters 2 and 3 review the history of developments in education and training for adult and working life, showing how 'new right' politics came to emphasise minimalist notions of competence and citizenship, and how these minimal versions of both concepts complemented each other in policies and programmes in Britain. Are they appropriate to the changing social context and situation of young adults? In the fourth chapter, the dynamics of social change are illustrated with reference to images and metaphors of transition and to ways in which these have changed over time. Chapter 5 presents some case histories of winners and losers in transition which, in Chapter 6, are set in the broader context of recent research into changing structures of opportunity and the 'risk' experienced by young people. These chapters highlight the effects of fragmented and individualised transitions on the life-course and demonstrate the need for maximal versions of both citizenship and competence if social cohesion, economic well-being and advancement of the democratic state are to be ensured. Further insights into minimal and maximal models of competence and citizenship are drawn from European comparisons in the last chapter. Finally, salient features of approaches to post-compulsory education and training which would foster maximal versions of competence and citizenship are outlined.

The overall thesis is that the workplace cannot continue to drive developments in posts-compulsory education, as the dominant source of values, standards and the curriculum. Having work-related competences is necessary but not sufficient preparation for being an effective member of society. An effective education for citizenship thus incorporates work preparation as an essential element. No longer merely an adjunct to the work-related curriculum, education for citizenship becomes the larger category. The goals of learning must derive from broader frameworks providing learners with the means and capacities for interpreting experience and for acting in the wider social world, while understanding the sources of diversity and differentiation within it. Furthermore, policies for alleviating the 'problems' of transitions to adult life, whether 'welfare to work' or extending higher education participation, must be based on more holistic analyses of social dynamics. As well as providing individual learning support, they must include measures which help to change the social and material conditions which stretch many young people beyond their individual capacities to cope unaided and which can defeat and ultimately exclude.

1 Education, work and citizenship: beyond the work-related curriculum

By the turn of the Century, most young adults in the developed world will continue in some form of education and training until their early 20s. New technology will have transformed work to the point where many intermediate skill jobs will have disappeared. The new structure of the workforce will have a stratum of jobs demanding high levels of intellectual skill, competence and flexibility, and a large, mobile sector of casualised labour, at all skill levels, operating by selling their services by contract.

How will young adults 'make their way', achieving their personal goals and fulfilling their social obligations, in this new scenario? Many will not achieve economic independence until their mid twenties, yet will have loosened the ties with their family of origin and established new households and in many cases their own families. The trends leading to this scenario are already firmly established. In the developed world the expansion of post-compulsory education has already contributed to the emergence of 'post-adolescence' as a life stage, in which young people have an ambiguous or 'in-between' status, and post-school enrolment in education is continuing to increase world-wide.

This book has its origins in studies of the life experiences of young adults in Britain and related research into the situation of their counterparts in Germany. Data have been provided by surveys and biographical interviews with young people from all walks of life. Adults who relate to young people on a day to day basis in the workplace, college or community have also contributed their views on the challenges faced by young adults in transition and on the support available to them in the forms of guidance, access to education and training, social support services and financial assistance.

These studies show the need to rethink what gaining adult status means, and to develop policies which both promote and support resourcefulness, personal achievement and social contribution in what could otherwise become an extended period of 'floundering' in in-between roles and indeterminate status:

> Angela is 21. She left home at the age of 17 and has been living on her own since then, in a shared flat. When she found difficulty in getting a job, she went on a number of training schemes which offered clerical and retail placements. None of these has provided long term opportunities, as she either disliked the work or was not kept on when the placement ended. She has now been unemployed for more than twelve months. She feels that she has wasted a lot of time and must now take steps to improve her qualifications and establish a career. She intends to enrol in a Further Education college to follow an Office Practice course. Despite the setbacks, she remains confident about her abilities and future prospects.

> Colin is 22. He originally intended to leave school at 16 to pursue his interest in working as a photographer but was persuaded by friends to stay on to do A levels. He went on to university immediately after completing his A levels to do a social science degree. He then spent some time travelling with a friend, as he had no idea of what types of work he wanted to pursue. He eventually took a job as a company salesman, which he disliked and left after less than a year. He is now unemployed, living at home and helping his parents with their business. He has no clear intentions or expectations about his future.

While these examples are typical of the experiences of many young adults in Britain, they are not the symptoms of a uniquely British disease. The experience of lengthy periods of 'floundering' is shared by young adults throughout the advanced industrialised nations. *Martina*, from Germany, provides another example:

> *Martina* finished Hauptschule, and was then unemployed for three months before joining a domestic science school for six months. She started an apprenticeship as a sales assistant but left after three months, bored with the work and unable to make friends. After another three months without work, she was offered a place on a training scheme, after which she began another apprenticeship, this time as a hairdresser, only to leave when the 'meister' left. She then gave up the idea of training altogether and took on unskilled work in a food-processing plant.

The case of Martina illustrates the power of relationships in the decisions young people take about education, training and work. These dimensions are often neglected in studies of career patterns. There is a need to take a more holistic view of young adults' experience. In developmental perspectives the process of transition to adulthood is a complex one involving three central psycho-social processes - the three 'I's of Identity, Intimacy and Independence, as defined by Merriam (1984)

During adolescence, young adults try to establish their own identity, experimenting within the peer group and outside it, to resolve identity confusion and arrive at a sense of wholeness and uniqueness as a separate person. Sense of identity involves moving away from self-centredness towards being able to see a place for oneself in a wider social context. Moving outwards from the family into the relationships and challenges of the wider world, experiencing people with different ideas and experiences from our own are all central to this process. The pace of such development is highly variable, and identity confusion is never resolved for some.

Intimacy, held by Erikson (1968) as the central growth task of young adulthood, depends to a large extent on the ways in which identities have taken shape. Real capacity for intimacy is only present when there is a sense of security about one's own boundaries. Only then is personal identity not threatened by intimacy. Intimacy experienced within the confines of family life gives way, often through experimentation and experience, to the mature forms of intimacy based on mutual valuing and free choice.

Independence is often construed in its economic sense, as standing on one's own feet financially. In young adulthood, independence is achieved gradually on a number of fronts. Young people establish values and beliefs of their own and make their own choices. Eventually most leave home, either permanently or for extended periods. This growing independence goes hand in hand with the process of establishing separate identities and eventually new intimacies.

How do people learn to be citizens? This begs several fundamental questions. How, first of all, do people learn to be adults, what kinds of adults do they learn to be and how do their experiences in the family, school, work and community contribute to this?

Do social learning processes in these domains produce 'passive knowers', contributing to reproduction of a society in which an active minority dominates a passive majority? Or do they produce adults who feel competent, confident and able to participate in shaping the direction of change? What is the role of the citizen in a democracy, and how does this fit with various visions and versions of the 'good society'?

Citizenship: a contested concept

The role of the citizen derives from the meanings associated with citizenship.

In examining the concept of citizenship from a philosophical standpoint, McLaughlin (1992) declares it to be 'full of ambiguities and tension', with different interpretations related to social and political positions and fundamental philosophical issues associated with any attempts to educate for citizenship.

McLaughlin identifies four features of citizenship: identity, virtues, political involvement and social requisites for citizenship. Each of these four features may be interpreted in 'minimal' or 'maximal' ways. 'Minimal' interpretations emphasise civil and legal status, rights and responsibilities, arising from membership of a community or society. The good citizen is law-abiding, public-spirited, exercises political involvement through voting for representatives. Citizenship is gained when civil and legal status is granted. 'Maximal' interpretations, by contrast, entail consciousness of self as a member of a shared democratic culture, emphasise participatory approaches to political involvement and consider ways in which social disadvantage can undermine citizenship, by denying people full participation in society in any significant sense. The maximal interpretation is reflected in the Speaker's Commission Report:

> The challenge to our society in the late twentieth century is to create conditions where all who wish to become actively involved, can understand and participate, can influence, persuade and campaign and whistle blow and in the making of decisions can work together for the common good

(1990, p.xvi)

At the other pole, minimal interpretations are reflected in government policies which have attempted to redefine citizenship in terms of individual consumer rights. Poverty and inequality act as barriers to the exercise of citizenship in either sense. As Lister (1991) says, it is not possible to divorce the rights and responsibilities which are supposed to unite citizens from the inequalities of power and wealth that divide them.

Citizenship has different meanings according to cultural and political identity, according to race, gender, class and personal biography. Citizenship is thus socially constructed and invokes a set of meanings, values and assumptions about the nation and political society:

> Citizenship is a form of cultural production ..... the making of citizens must be understood as an ideological process through which we experience ourselves as well as our relations to others and the world within a complex and often contradictory system of representations and images

(Giroux, 1989, p.16)

In operating at the interface between the personal and the political, citizenship involves the tensions between individualism and the need to make one's own way in life, and the public good. In versions which take the rights of the individual as their starting point, the obligation is to sustain and to protect the individual, assuring to each individual his or her rights, compatible with the good order of society; leaving individuals free, as far as possible, to pursue their own projects. Those who subscribe to minimal versions often see the mechanisms of the market as the means to achieve this equilibrium between the individual and the public good. In maximal versions, market regulation is seen as inadequate to achieve this. Citizenship requires a sense of community (Quicke, 1992) and 'shared autonomy'. Norman (1992) argues that the concept of shared autonomy recognises that lives are fundamentally affected by many factors beyond individual control, and that the only way of achieving effective control is through democratic institutions. Furthermore individual action may be more rational and autonomous if influenced by the judgement of others as well as one's own. Shared autonomy therefore goes hand in hand with pursuit of personal projects, and links individualism with the 'public good'.

Education for Citizenship

These differing notions of citizenship carry different implications for education. Education for citizenship in its minimal interpretation requires only induction into basic knowledge of institutionalised rules concerning rights and obligations. Maximal interpretations require education which develops critical and reflective abilities and enables capacities for self-determination and shared autonomy to grow.

In Britain, education for citizenship was receiving little serious attention at the time the Commission on Citizenship was established, with the Rt. Hon. Bernard Weatherill MP, Speaker of the House of Commons, as patron (1988). The Commission identified a threat to democracy in an increasingly commercial society, where insecurity and sense of isolation and powerlessness become the everyday experience of growing numbers of individuals, and asked whether we are, as a society, creating conditions of the 'mass society of mutually antagonistic individuals, easy prey to despotism'.

The Commission produced what Frances Morrell (a member of the Commission) termed a traditional British analysis of citizenship, following the classic approach of Marshall (1950) based on civil, political and social elements, and emphasising individual freedom, rights to participate in the exercise of political power and the right to share 'to the full' in the social heritage. Rights and responsibilities were seen as standing 'in their own right' as Morrell (1991) puts it, and not necessarily as a quid pro quo arrangement, a deal between the individual and society.

The Commission's work had some influence on the re-emergence of education for citizenship as a cross-curriculum theme in the framing of the National Curriculum. Citizenship was one of five non-mandatory cross-curricular themes identified by the National Curriculum Council, the others being careers education and guidance, economic awareness, health education and environmental education. Schools were guided to teach these themes largely through the mandatory core and other foundation subjects. The National Curriculum Council Report (1990) which elaborated this theme emphasised increasing diversity, Europeanisation and multiculturalism, and put forward a wide range of approaches through which, it states, the foundation can be laid for 'positive, participative citizenship'. As McLaughlin shows, there are some aspects of the Report which can be read in maximal ways as well as many which lend themselves to minimalist readings. For example, maximal interpretations are suggested by the references to awareness of political structures and processes and 'independence of thought on social and moral issues', based on consideration of questions of diversity, justice and inequality in society.

While no explicit statement is made of underlying values, a clear value position is discernible in the emphasis on duties and responsibilities and on the pluralist conception of society. The latter is reflected in the emphasis on diversity as a source of tensions and the implicit assumption that these tensions can be resolved by consensus around a set of shared values. There is little acknowledgement, for example, of the position that power is contested and that society is made up of competing interest groups with differentials of power and influence operating at all levels. The emphasis is on normative concepts of the 'good citizen' rather than on critical participation in social and political processes. This represents a packaging of social and political values as though they were part of an agreed syllabus for an uncontested subject, despite its apparent breadth and scope.

The Report of the independent National Commission on Education, 'Learning to Succeed' also adopted a pluralistic model of society combined with treatments of citizenship which are more open to maximal readings, but also failed to acknowledge the contested conceptual frameworks within which notions of citizenship are discussed and operationalised.

Morrell highlighted the contrast between the way academics philosophise about meanings of citizenship with the apparent unity of views of young people surveyed by Richardson (1990).

> It is unusual to find wide consensus on any issue. Yet in this study, there was one issue which united virtually everyone across the social spectrum. From those who had left school with few qualifications to those in University or

beyond, there was a strong call for more teaching of the issues surrounding citizenship in schools ......'

(Richardson, 1990, p.35)

The Speaker's Commission emphasised that the skills of citizenship need to be learned and that considerations of citizenship should be incorporated in education at all levels, from the earliest years, through further and adult education, and also in professional education and training.

In practice, citizenship education is little in evidence at any level. While nominally present in the form of a cross-curricular theme associated with the National Curriculum in schools, evidence (Whitty et al 1996) has shown that these themes are 'submerged' within the strongly framed National Curriculum subjects, with very limited opportunities for pupils to relate the themes to everyday lives:

> Very few pupils had heard of the term 'economic and industrial understanding' or thought they were being taught any. The findings were similar for education for citizenship except in one school which had a specific citizenship module as part of a PSE (Personal and Social Education) module. (p.62)

In post-16 education and training, citizenship education per se has reduced since the virtual demise of liberal studies, although the encouragement of 'balancing studies' of various kinds for those following primarily academic routes may be seen as an attempt to develop learners' ability to inquire within and through a broader set of frameworks and perspectives than previously narrowly specialised programmes allowed or encouraged. Such approaches have been beset with problems of not being taken seriously, often being seen as timetable-fillers by students and some teachers. In 1996 proposals for reform of post-16 education have again incorporated moral education and citizenship as adjuncts and side issues to the main business of educating for work. On page 125 (of 136 pages) the Dearing report makes reference to the spiritual and moral dimension of 16-19 education.

> Life entails a continuous series of moral judgements and decisions. In work, the need to face ethical issues arises constantly ..... The moral and spiritual dimensions are as relevant to vocational as to academic courses ..... .
>
> Schools and colleges can and do transmit a common culture and common standards of citizenship. But the evidence of the times we live in suggests that there is merit in re-emphasising the need to address moral and spiritual issues and to build the public and private virtues of citizenship and community.

(Dearing, 1996, pp. 125-126)

These approaches to citizenship and citizenship education have not moved far from normative approaches based on the social dynamics of the 50s and

60s. There is some enlargement, to make them more 'inclusive' of diversity of background and experience, but are they adequate for the fragmented and polarised, sometimes marginalised, life situations emerging for many young people as they encounter blocked opportunities, reduced access to resources and social exclusion in their endeavours to negotiate their way to adulthood? (Williamson, 1996). In a wider European context, where social exclusion and citizenship have become intertwined as primary policy concerns, it is increasingly recognised that the social processes that are shaping lives reflect the complex interactions of social structures with the actions and behaviours of young people themselves - the interplay of structure and agency in unprecedented circumstances of perceived risk and uncertainty. How far is it the operation of differentials of power and cultural capital which bring stability or instability to the life course? How far do social rights play a part in shaping the life course, how far do individual capabilities contribute to success in negotiating uncharted waters?

Schooling may be promulgating 'passive knower' models in providing information-based civics education on rights and duties of citizenship in a democracy; or it may be giving openings for the 'movers and shakers' of academic or social elites to practise their skills in a safe institutional environment. Education for citizenship may become ineffectively minimalist, or seriously controversial when maximal in approach. The institutional educator committed to maximal versions of citizenship is thus potentially caught in contradictions of a fundamental kind. While some educators may seek 'space' in the curriculum for approaches which effectively focus on structural questions of power and social location, and the social processes which shape life chances unequally, these understandings are likely to be at odds with some of the normative assumptions on which the structures and processes of schooling themselves continue to rest and which imply different models of citizenship and citizenship education.

For some of those who subscribe to maximal versions of citizenship, education for citizenship is better tackled outside the formal structures of schooling, in non-formal youth or community organisations in which aims, values and structures are more congruent with the processes being learned. The danger is that this may marginalise citizenship education, open its proponents to accusations of 'indoctrination', and limit exposure to these forms of education to the voluntary users of the organisations in question.

The contribution of youth and community work

Youth and community work in any society will reflect the development of that society, historically, politically and economically. In developing countries, for example, youth and community work has aims and priorities which often centre on self-reliance, citizenship, self-employment and 'development' skills. A typical example of youth policy objectives is cited by Kukler (1987, p 149):

a. The youth is made familiar with the social, economic, cultural and political objectives of the Government.

b. The spirit of co-operation and understanding amongst youth is promoted.

c. The youth is enabled to acquire the necessary skills for development activities.

d. The youth is put in a position to play an active part within the national economy.

e. The youth are developed into responsible and responsive citizens.

f. The spirit of self-help, self-confidence and independence is instilled in them.

g. The youth should be prepared to defend their countries' freedom and independence if the need arises.

In the former Soviet Union and Eastern Europe of the recent past, youth organisations were closely controlled as part of the state machinery. They played a central role in pursuit of state objectives, in a context in which there was a broader conception of the scope of education with overt social objectives permeating the curriculum in every sector. Non-formal provision in the USA and Western Europe has been provided through a wide variety of forms of service and institution, but with a common general aim of developing individual maturity and community involvement. While youth and community work in the West has suffered from a position perceived as peripheral to the business of 'mainstream education', in the Eastern part of Europe non-formal education had a high priority, ensuring socialisation and social control of the young along Communist Party lines (Fearey and Lalor, 1991). However, state control meant that the exercise of freedom and responsibility were not assured (Marsland, 1991).

The Youth Service curriculum in Britain shifted from a focus on physical fitness and the promotion of family values, to an emphasis on personal resources of 'body, mind and spirit' and good citizenship in the post-war years. This need to develop citizenship was highlighted in the Albemarle Report of 1960 and the concept of social education was brought to the fore.

With the Milson-Fairbairn Report in 1969, a new emphasis was given to more active roles for young people in society and for political education to form an explicit part of social education. In 1982, the Thompson Report saw the role of youth work as affirming and involving individual young people. This Report had a central concern with alienation (which it saw as often leading to juvenile crime and drug abuse); unemployment; homelessness; the hardship of life in the inner cities and in rural areas. The need to counter racism and sexism, and the importance of work with those with disabilities was highlighted. Much emphasis was also placed on greater participation by young people in all levels of the service and the report reasserted the central place of political and social education in youth work, in unequivocal terms.

The Youth Service, in the early 1990s, was called on to justify its continued existence by making explicit its unique contribution to the education and development of young people. It was challenged to say what it could do that other agencies cannot. In parallel with this, it has been increasingly constrained by reducing resources and central governmental interventions, which have required it, through the National Youth Agency, to identify a core curriculum with measurable outcomes.

In all of this it is possible to see common strands and at the same time significant changes in the content of youth work practice. The emphasis on good citizenship remains, but the attention to 'issues-based' work in equal opportunities, health education, and environmental issues has grown. Again, the prevailing economic climate and the introduction of ideas from commerce and industry and governmental pressure caused the service to prioritise its work and to reconsider the age groups to be 'targeted'.

In 1990, the National Youth Bureau suggested the following as a mission statement for the Youth Service:

> The intent of the Youth Service is to assist young people to make sense of the personal, social and political issues which affect their lives; to promote young people's self-awareness, self-confidence and competence in relationships; to encourage the making of decisions and choices (for example, education and training); to support the development of independent judgement by young people and their ability to express their opinions and values; and to advocate with and for young people the defence and extension of opportunities and choices available to them.
>
> (National Youth Bureau, 1990, p.35)

The Thompson Report and 1990 National Youth Bureau Report were clearly maximal in their positions on social and political education, emphasising the need to consider social inequalities, and taking as their starting points the recognition of both diversity and inequality. Citizenship education in this approach must enable young people to understand the social processes which produce and reproduce inequalities and to see how they can act from the social positions they hold.

While the Youth and Community Service in England and Wales has long held values associated with citizenship at its heart, the extent to which it attracts and engages young people reduces dramatically after the age of 16. Many young people cease their participation in youth organisations by their mid-teens and do not experience the service in the way envisaged (Evans 1994). For the majority of young people, their understanding of social processes comes through their day to day experiences inside, outside, and beyond schooling and their access to the transformative kinds of experiential learning embodied in the best of Youth and Community practice is very limited.

Increasingly diversified patterns of experience after sixteen mean that transitions are fractured for some and others lose their way. More institutionalised frameworks can provide greater social support, but can become over-institutionalised in a way which is rejected by young people trying to find their autonomy and independence, as the experience in Denmark has shown. There, an EC Task Group (Chisholm and Bergereet 1991) reported that young people's interests appeared no longer to tally with the philosophy underlying policy, in which 'organised' cultural life was seen as a means of promoting social integration, alongside extended education. The looser, more ad hoc arrangements of the British kind may create a less institutionalised space for independence and autonomy to be exercised, but with increasing risk of marginalisation and social exclusion for those unfavourably positioned and with few resources on which they can call.

Competence and Citizenship

What is the place of competence, the new mantra of the 1990s, in these processes? Competence is certainly implied in both maximal and minimal versions of citizenship. To operate as a full citizen in society, an individual has to have the legal and civic status of citizen, with accompanying rights and obligations, the will and motivation to contribute to the 'common good' and the knowledge and skills to participate effectively. This includes understanding of diversity, difference and the contested nature of what constitutes the 'common good' together with the skills and dispositions to engage in dialogue and peaceful conflict resolution. While this refers to competence in 'skills' of citizenship itself, broader forms of social and economic competence are also implied in becoming a citizen. Approaches to development for adulthood and citizenship may emphasise:

- Insight and identity formation
- Self awareness and autonomy

- Social roles, power and policy
- Competence, skills and dispositions.

Citizenship has increasingly been framed instrumentally as an adjunct to employment with an emphasis on narrowly-based competences and skills. This is encapsulated in Mead's (1986) view that work is the most important of our social obligations and that 'the operational definition of (social) citizenship places emphasis on 'learning enough to be employable', and on 'activity and competence'.

Like citizenship, competence is a value-laden word. It is difficult to be 'against' competence. The concept is also socially constructed, taking on different meanings according to social location and is used to support particular ideological positions. Norris (1991) distinguishes between behaviourist, generic and cognitive constructs of competence. Behavioural interpretations of competence are performance related. That is, they equate competence with the ability to perform a range of tasks to predetermined standards. Such approaches to competence are criticised for their narrowness, for confusing competence with performance and for ignoring the underlying capacities needed for change. These can be considered minimal interpretations of the concept. Like minimal interpretations of the citizenship concept, they do not imply any need for critical, reflective abilities.

They are typified in Britain in the approaches to occupational competence shaping much of the discourse about post-school education and training in the 1990s. It has been argued elsewhere (Blackman and Evans, 1994) that this minimalist interpretation of competence serves the objectives of curriculum modernisers, who have put an emphasis on state intervention to achieve an enterprise economy, through a free market where access to knowledge and skill is 'democratised'.

Moore (1987) argues that the labour market has been redefined in terms of the rationale of competences, collected together as units, elements and range statements, the function being to 'measure the individual against the ideal worker which the skills matrix represents' (p.230). The concept of competence thus becomes essentially technical, and omits the social meanings and social relations of work. Moreover, as Jones and Moore (1993) argue, its 'concern with transparency both rejects the contextual and discursive character of social competence and presents its own models as simple reflections of the real rather than as constructs' (p.395). The individualised, technical approach to competence de-skills individuals in terms of competences acquired within the informal localised networks of everyday life (Giddens, 1991) and thus effectively disempowers them. In this sense it is best understood as part of the broader framework of regulation and control in modern societies. Others such as Issitt (1995) argue that approaches which equate competence with performance are essentially retrospective, reflecting and reinforcing the status quo and therefore reproducing structural inequalities.

Generic and cognitive constructs of competence, by contrast, emphasise broad clusters of abilities which are conceptually linked. They involve an underlying generative capacity reflected in general ability to co-ordinate resources necessary for successful adaptation (Norris, 1991). These may be seen as maximal interpretations. They imply the need for critical reflective learning and emphasise the development of self-efficacy and shared autonomy. Reflective learning is considered essential if competence is to become future oriented, that is, able to develop the skills of the future (Brown, 1994, Wellington, 1987) rather than tied to the performance of narrowly specified tasks. Eraut (1993) also refers to broad capability, rather than narrowly defined competence, as being crucial.

In the person-centred professions Issitt (1995) has shown that 'equal opportunities' provide a testing ground for the development of competence-based procedures. She identifies ways in which occupations governed by discourse and action on equal opportunities, such as youth and community work, have developed an holistic notion of competence to avoid contradictions inherent in adopting the technical individualistic model which reproduces structural inequalities.

These contradictions and tensions have contributed to mounting pressure for a move towards maximal, or more holistic constructs of competence in education and training.

Contextualised learning and vocationalism

Competence can be seen as an outcome of learning which has been 'contextualised', that is learning which has taken place in an environment similar to that in which the learner seeks to practise. In Bernstein's (1981) terms, competence involves knowing the rules that enable you to produce appropriate responses in a particular context.

There is some evidence that learning environments which encourage social interchange provide a context for learners to arrive at higher levels of cognition through the structuring of their own understandings, thus reinforcing the importance of social practice (Habermas, 1970; Quicke, 1992) and underlining the contextual basis for knowledge.

What vocationalism, whether in its broader or narrower forms, has done is to appropriate a form of contextualised learning in pursuit of its goals. It employs relatively narrow conceptions of competence which come from, and reflect, a distinctly instrumental interpretation of social needs, related to industry, the economy and international competitiveness. Associated with this 'force' of instrumentalism in education and training are agencies and interests represented by the Training and Enterprise Councils, the former Department of Employment and employers' organisations, whose efforts have been directed towards promotion of work-related curricula at all levels of education.

The workplace, rather than the academy, becomes the 'pivotal curriculum authority' (Sedunary, 1996). Where the workplace has been defined in terms of competences, learning becomes narrowly task-oriented.

The workplace as ultimate curriculum authority also requires outlooks in citizens and workers compatible with underlying political and economic objectives and the evolving structures of work. While education, historically, has contributed to the development of outlooks in young people consistent with their likely future level in the workforce - independence and creativity for the upper strata, passivity, dependency and conformity for the lower (Bowles and Gintis, 1976) - passivity and dependence at any level of the workforce are now seen to be incompatible with successful achievement of economic goals. A 'settlement' has developed around the goal of modernisation, according to Avis (1993), who observes an alignment of the various stakeholders in work-related education despite underlying conceptual and ideological differences, an emerging 'affinity between post-Fordist analysis and curriculum modernisers' (p 265). The changed social and economic context demands new attitudes and dispositions in the pool of labour. Creativity and enterprise are emphasised in Government policy, 'hurrah' words according to Coffield (1990). A more detailed look at the language of statements of policy in the White Papers of the '80s and '90s reveals three elements of this appropriate outlook: self reliance, initiative, readiness to adapt and learn new skills. While educators and trainers have been exhorted to enable young adults to understand wealth creation and create futures for themselves (eg MSC, 1982; DE/DES 1991) the limits to this self-determination have been also apparent in the policy stances of the various government agencies involved. These have discouraged help being given to trainees in Government schemes in acquiring the conceptual and critical skills which would enable them to understand their situation and its causes and possibly generate some alternative futures not envisaged within government policy! (Watts, 1983; Gleeson, 1990). 'Submissive man' has progressively been replaced by 'conforming flexible person' (Ball, 1990).

In broader forms, the dualism inherent in the separation of education and work is replaced by an 'integrated concept' of vocationalism, one in which work and education are collapsed into one another. The new workplace reintegrates intellectual and manual labour and 'key competencies' may come to embrace some circumscribed intellectual skills in the application of knowledge and understanding or in a focus on generic 'know-how'.

Contextualised vocational learning and wider social purposes

Contextualised vocational learning need not be so confined and confining. Individuals learn conceptually as well as practically through contextualised learning, and some, perhaps most, learn better in this way (Carmichael, 1992, p.60). In its broader forms it can also embrace development of the values which underlie and motivate social participation.

In Dewey's (1916) conceptualisation, work is any purposeful activity, which both gives service to others and contributes to personal growth by engaging and developing the creative powers of the individual. This conceptualisation embraces work of all kinds, paid and unpaid, and breaks down the divide between a 'liberal education' which fosters personal and moral growth and 'vocational education' which prepares for paid employment. It values work of all kinds as the point of connection between individuals' energies and purposes and those of the wider society (Chanan, 1976). It thus links the concepts of worker and citizen, since work is both a virtuous activity and a sphere of social practice which connects the individual with wider social purposes. Identities and moral purposes are rooted and tied up in it. The implications for the form and content of vocational education and training are considerable if Gramscian ideas, paraphrased by Entwhistle (1979), drive and frame the curriculum:

> To have a vocation goes beyond mastery of the technical skill and knowledge required to complete an industrial or professional task competently. It also entails an awareness of moral obligation, an appreciation of the political and economic implications of a job of work and of the aesthetics of production. (p.130)

Awareness and appreciation are developed over time, and become part of the shared understandings and values of the workplace. Lupton illustrates some 'shared understandings' in his account of his experiences as an apprentice engineer in the 1960s.

> To work too quickly was to be labelled a 'teararse' and to be at least partly shut out from the friendly give and take of the shop...... . It was also regarded as a breach of workshop custom to be too much a 'scrounger'. The man who persistently dodged work and whose output fell below what was generally considered 'decent' became an object of ridicule. Equally, ... the man who produced shoddy work lost status in the shop... so workshop custom was reinforced by the value placed on a high standard of workmanship ..... .' (p.2).

As well as highlighting the social processes at work, this short extract also hints at the moral and aesthetic content of the shared understandings. Work orientations and values initially developed through home and schooling, are thus refined or refocused through the social relations of the workplace and through membership of communities of practice. The same applies to citizenship orientations and values, in which the 'communities of practice' include, but extend far beyond, the workplace.

Georg Kerschensteiner, founder of the German Vocational Education and Training system, in his prize essay on the question 'How is our youth best to be educated for citizenship in the years between the completion of elementary education and conscription?' (1900), started with the simple but powerful point that the aims of education and their realisation start with the role the state allots to its citizens. His ideas not only revolutionised German vocational education and training but also had widespread influence throughout continental Europe. The aims of education were to be to make people capable of attaining both the general 'calling' (Bestimmung) of morality and the special calling of usefulness. Education was to be concerned with moral, intellectual and technical training, with technical instruction the first stage towards the ultimate goal of education.

According to Kerschensteiner, every school and training institute (including elementary schools) should be given three defined tasks:

1. Vocational education or at least preparation for vocational education.
2. Making this vocational education a moral education.
3. Teaching the moral value of the community in which the trade is to be carried out.

Kerschensteiner met Dewey in the course of travels to America and was surprised to discover the similarity of thinking. Both emphasised the development of the social being in and through all forms of work, and Kerschensteiner saw group work on shared tasks as the focus for this. He also saw the period of apprenticeship (15-18) as the optimum age to *begin* the process of citizenship education. Young people who had embarked on continuation education as part of a long term apprenticeship were beginning to gain a greater awareness of their role in society and the significance of work in the functioning of the wider society. This growing awareness was linked with their direct experience of the practice of their trade and contributing to their 'keep'. Experience of working in a social group on purposeful, shared tasks of a practical nature, was a central feature of learning for citizenship:

> By doing this type of work the individual learns how to subordinate himself (sic) to others and how to help his weaker and less talented companions. Here,

too, he first comes to understand that his own interests can, and should, merge into the interests of others. The civic virtues of devotion and self-control grow out of this collective work, characterised by its well-thought-out plan and well-fitting order. Likewise, when the virtues of carefulness, conscientiousness, hard work and perseverance are employed in common service, they are transformed into altruistic virtues. This joint work provides, then, fruitful soil for civic instruction in such subjects as community life......, the common tasks and duties in the employer's workshop, on the farm, in the parish, in the borough and in the state.

(Kerschensteiner, 1911, pp 52-4)

Competence and citizenship are thus intertwined in the notions of work and education as social practices. Social practices may be structured in ways which generate and sustain forms of consciousness which perpetuate subordination of social groups along class, gender or ethnic lines. Or they may generate and sustain group solidarities and collective struggles for change. If citizenship implies competence, then competence needs to be developed in a way which is compatible with the wider requirements of citizenship. This includes competence, at the individual level, which maximises prospects of achieving economic independence. At the collective level, maximal interpretations involve shared autonomy and ability to participate in the political processes which influence the social and economic scenarios of the future. Competence is thus associated with certain forms of identity, values and social participation, all of which are central elements of citizenship. In the late 20th century context, much of what passes as 'education for adult life' can be seen to be more about 'sponsoring individuals acting in support of their own sectionalised interests' (Gleeson, 1990) than it is about promoting understanding of the relationships between individuals and the wider society.

It is a restricted 'independence', characterised by ownership of marketable skills and attitudes of enterprise, which is promoted in the post-16 initiatives of the 80's and 90's. This is far removed from the concept of independence implied in maximal concepts of citizenship.

..... In this sleight of thinking, where education for work becomes education for the broader spheres of adult life, and where instrumental intellect is detached from a more comprehensive orientation to social practice, adult life and citizenship themselves inevitably become human experience to be perceived and approached instrumentally

(Sedunary 1996)

Such one-sided instrumental interpretations of social need lead to one-dimensional human development. As Skilbeck et al observed in 1986, the approaches to vocationalism have to be assessed in terms of their adequacy to meet the task of preparing a generation for new structures of work and leisure:

> At the very least we must be assessing these programmes against social dynamics ... . This calls for a rather more powerful and comprehensive analysis, or response to analyses, of the place of youth, its wants, preferences and needs and social trends, than we seem to be witnessing in many OECD countries, UK included ... . Training programmes may transmit neither the broader initial skill training needed for the workplace of the future nor the varied life skills which are essential for survival in the modern world and active, responsible and fulfilling participation in society (p 65).

Both the definitions and the processes by which government purports to develop independence and creativity were criticised by those who claim that the reform of education was the way to prepare young adults for the future, not the construction of an alternative system hurriedly erected on crudely conceived work-based tasks, a system in which the trainee is treated as a 'bundle of limited motivations with a potential of skill ownership' (Skilbeck et al p 177).

One way of analysing programmes against social dynamics is through comparative analysis. The author's comparisons of experiences of samples of young people in England[1] and Germany (Evans and Heinz 1994) have shown how cultural assumptions about the ways in which young people should be prepared for adult and working life through a combination of education training and work are reflected in different concepts of youth and young adulthood. Germany, for example, has a strongly institutionalised system of preparation for work and adult life based on 'anticipatory socialisation' in extended full-time education or apprenticeship. In other words, whichever route they take after compulsory schooling, young adults are prepared for future responsibility as citizens and workers through a broad curriculum which includes social studies, political education and modern language education. Other industrialised countries such as USA and Japan also have extended periods of anticipatory socialisation, through schooling to age 18 as the norm, followed by mass participation in various forms of post-secondary education, often combined with part-time work.

In the post-communist countries of Central and Eastern Europe there is now

---

[1] The studies cited focused on labour markets in England. As the Scottish system and modes of provision differ substantially from the English, conclusions drawn specifically from the studies refer only to England, not to Britain as a whole.

'A general conviction that post-compulsory education must necessarily include the political dimension. Its function should be to provide a reliable knowledge of democratic institutions and to promote positive attitudes towards the full exercise of civic rights and obligations by all citizens' (J J Tomiak, 1995, p 52).

England's mixed and divided model of post-16 provision, in which young people may follow academic education, or a wide range of vocational education or work-based training programmes, does not give the strongly institutionalised framework for transition which is provided by the German or North American systems. This has meant that many young people are closer to the world of work and to 'adult responsibilities' at an early age. Anglo-German comparisons showed that in each career trajectory, from higher education through to unemployment/unskilled work, young people in England were entering the labour market at least two years ahead of their German counterparts and were experiencing higher degrees of responsibility and remuneration.

Normative tasks which define transition to adult status and its recognition are thus defined more broadly in Germany than in England, with citizenship as an adjunct to employment implied in both. In Central and Eastern Europe they are linked with 're-education' of the population, with citizenship central to the curriculum.

Is all this being overtaken by the social dynamics of global change? In all societies young adults are today experiencing uncertain status and are dependent upon state and parental support for longer periods than would have been the case a generation ago. Possible pathways at the end of schooling have diversified, and young people have to find their own ways forward and their own values in education, consumption, politics, work and family life. Achieving adult status comes at different times within these domains and young people face status inconsistency. They may for example be supporting a family while on a grant, or still in training. Or they may hold responsible positions in work while remaining in their family of origin, still the child in the household but supporting other members financially.

These different patterns of life and work can be viewed as manifestations of the emergence of the 'risk society', as portrayed by Ulrich Beck. Traditional socialising agencies such as the extended and nuclear family, the church and the school no longer act as agencies of social reproduction; they no longer channel individuals into predetermined niches and levels of society. Rather, it is argued, an infinite range of courses of action has opened up for people. This results in increased levels of risk for all, the 'risk society' (Beck 1992).

All approaches to education for citizenship and transition to adult status rest on a particular view of society. If curricula continue to be driven by normative definitions of tasks and capabilities which ignore the operation of power differentials in society, citizenship education will be framed by the assumptions contained therein. If they subscribe to the view that structures determine outcomes, with minimal scope for individual agency, citizenship education will focus more on understanding power relations and collective action. If they recognise the cultural production that citizenship entails, they will focus on the ideological processes and the values, meanings and assumptions themselves. If they continue to be driven by the dictates of work and to interpret citizenship as merely an adjunct to them, they will 'provide no alternative framework for interpretative grasping of and acting upon the world as a social whole'. (Sedunary 1996)

While work provides a point of connection between individual purposes and the wider society, the dangers of linking employment with citizenship rights and obligations are spelt out by Dahrendorf:

> Citizenship is a social contract, generally valid for all members; work is a private contract...... . For when the general rights of citizenship are made dependent on people entering into the private relations of employment, these lose their private and fundamentally voluntary characteristic. In an indirect but compelling manner, labour becomes forced labour. It is imperative that the obligations of citizenship are themselves general and public....'. (1996, p. 33).

These dangers become even more apparent when considered in the context of the post-fordist visions of the future of work outlined at the start of this chapter.

Historically, strong links between private relations of employment and the public obligations of citizenship have been encapsulated in the portrayal of young people as 'workers and citizens in training'. This portrayal fitted the purposes of post-war social reconstruction and, subsequently, the conditions of 'full employment' and high levels of absorption of young people into the labour market at 15 or 16 years of age.

This portrayal has given way to that of young people as producers and consumers and future wealth creators in the years of 'new right' government with some evidence of a swing back to recognition of the importance of citizenship, as reflected in the Speaker's Commission, and the National Commission on Education, and the manifesto of the newly elected Labour Government in 1997. Awareness of historical constructions of young people as 'workers and citizens in training' provides insights into the contemporary debate and, as McCulloch (1995) notes, may help to avoid 'reinventing wheels' and to appreciate the complexities of the social and economic factors involved.

2 Effective workers, good citizens? Legacies of the past

Employment, historically, was the main means by which young people became socially and economically integrated into the wider society. This transition took place at a relatively early age in Britain, in a stratified, socially reproductive way but the social processes involved were not, in themselves, seen as sufficient to produce effective 'worker-citizens'.

It was in the closing years of the 1939-45 war that both part-time day education and the non-formal youth services first developed into national systems of post-school provision, education and social support for the majority of young people who entered employment at 15.

Prior to the war, provision had been variable and patchy in both spheres. The pattern of part-time further education which emerged in the mid-1940s had its roots in the long established tradition of post-school education which had afforded opportunities, albeit on a limited scale, for apprentices to attend Mechanics Institutes during the day, or more usually the evening, in order to receive technical instruction related to their trade.

In the early 1900s, however, the ideal of universal access to education for young people in the early years of employment gained wide acceptance, eventually receiving official recognition and acceptance as a goal towards which a civilised society should aspire. It was underpinned, ostensibly, by concern over the vulnerability of youth and the damage to the developing mind which could be caused by entry into unrewarding or limited and repetitious forms of work. This view was encapsulated in the 1909 Consultative Committee Report of the Board of Education:

> Certain branches of machine production are being so organised as to make profitable the employment of boy and girl labour in processes which, while demanding some intelligence and previous school training, are in themselves non-educative and deadening to the mind .....

..... organised efforts are needed to counteract the hurtful effects of these new economic developments (p.6).

A model of 'continuation education' began to emerge which was quite different both in concept and in practice from that already established in the Mechanics Institutes. The concept of 'continuation education' for all young people was translated into a series of proposals for a national system of post-school education based on day continuation schools. The aims of such schools and their place in the educational system were outlined by Sir Michael Sadler in 1908. The schools were to prepare their pupils both for the duties of citizenship and the skills required for the 'breadwinning occupations'. The 1909 Consultative Paper presented a series of recommendations for day continuation education, later to be strengthened in the proposals of the Lewis Report (1917), and incorporated in the Education Act of 1918. The adoption of the concept of day continuation education for young workers had undoubtedly been influenced by the developments in Germany and Georg Kerschensteiner's work. A report on the German developments published by the British Board of Education in 1910 described the schools initiated in Munich as 'probably the most perfectly organised and perfectly equipped system of continuation schools in the world' (p.23). William Morris, British social reformer, was among the leading advocates of continuation education, linking 'manual training' with aesthetics and citizenship. He eventually found more fertile ground for expression of his ideas through Georg Kerschensteiner and the German movement, which extended compulsory continuation school attendance for vocational education throughout Germany through the 1919 Weimar Constitution.

The 1918 Act of Parliament in Britain laid on local authorities the duty to provide day continuation schools, and gave them the power to impose compulsory release and compulsory attendance on young people aged under 17. These measures failed to produce the national system envisaged for reasons of lack of compulsion on the authorities to use the powers given to them under the Act, reluctance of employers to release their young employees, inadequate staffing and facilities in the schools themselves and, finally and most importantly, the reduction of resources available for the programme during the economic depression of the 1920s. The programme was eventually postponed for an indefinite period.

However, some of the authorities decided to proceed with those programmes which had already been implemented, thereby affording opportunities for education on the day continuation model to a small proportion of the nation's young workers. Nevertheless, the number of young people receiving continued day education more than halved between

1921 and 1938. Evening courses were thus to remain the main route to self 'improvement' and qualification available to the young worker during the inter-war years.

In parallel with these movements, forms of educative provision based on alternative structures to those of the formal, statutory educational systems had emerged through the organisation of voluntary effort during the 19th Century, and gained momentum following the 1870 Education Act. The social reforms of the time, combined with the advances of industrialisation, had produced a marked reduction in working hours for young people in employment. The opportunity to make provision for use of the newly-found leisure time was seized on by commercialists and industrialists. The issue of the 'appropriate' use of leisure time by young people of the working classes rapidly became an issue of social concern. While unskilled young people were the prime source of anxiety, the gradual erosion of the traditional forms of support of 'masters' for their apprentices also presented a problem. Persistent suspicion of direct Government intervention in such matters led many of the evolving voluntary organisations to take 'youth work' to their heart.

Activities and movements designed to provide for constructive social activity for young people in employment emerged through the voluntary efforts of individuals and groups and, as Jeffs (1979) pointed out, many of the youth organisations so established immediately saw their work as extending far beyond that of simply filling the leisure time of the underprivileged young.

The resulting initiatives, which stemmed predominantly from middle and upper class social strata, were underpinned by a variety of motives. On the one hand, the altruistic desire to provide opportunities for worthwhile activity for those whose social environments were seen as limiting their choices and opportunities, and on the other, a self-protective desire to reduce the potential threat posed by the working classes by socialising young people into middle class values and ways of thinking, were both in evidence. The source of initiatives and the mixed motives which underpinned them were strongly reflected in the statements of tacit aims and purposes of the activities provided. Davies and Gibson (1967) observed that:

> Ensuring that the young grew into 'full Christian manliness', together with training them to be 'good citizens' and for 'responsible roles in society', all involved preparing the young to accept an economic, political and religious structure because it was there and because any disturbance of it would have endangered the position of those who controlled it. (p. 30)

At the same time there was evidence of genuine concern to develop the young 'to make them something more than they already were'. The welfare and social reforms at the turn of the century removed many of the remaining social rescue functions of youth work. This increased the marginality of youth work with, as Jeffs suggests, the less tangible social and spiritual dimensions being the only legitimate ground left to them. It is significant that youth work was not considered to be in any way associated with the educational services. Education of the young was seen as a process which takes place in the school, as distinct from processes of learning taking place in and through other agencies - a conception which still hampers the youth services a century later.

Major youth organisations emerging from the social circumstances and conditions outlined here, between 1860 and 1918 were the Army Cadet Force (1869), Boys' Brigade (1883), Church Lads' Brigade (1891), Boy Scouts (1907), Girl Guides (1910).

In the following years, the first indications of Government support emerged in the form of provision for local authorities to make allocations of small amounts of funding to youth work co-ordination and activity. Many of the initiatives involving local government intervention withered almost immediately, sharing a similar fate to that of the day continuation developments in the economic cutbacks of the early 1920s. However, the development of Juvenile Instruction Centres, created in response to the problems created by large scale unemployment, gave one clear and continuing indication of Government willingness to involve itself in the provision of facilities for youth, a sign which came to be associated with a marked trend towards Government intervention during the remainder of the inter-war years.

The voluntary movements were reflected, to some extent, within industry itself. Some larger companies, motivated by 'social conscience' or paternalistic concern for the welfare of their young employees, established their own programmes. Some, in response to the day continuation proposals, had established and maintained their own continuation schools. Cadbury, for example, established and ran continuation schools which were for a long time showpieces for industrial initiatives in supporting the education of young workers. In some companies, factory youth clubs were established, while in others special youth programmes were initiated.

1939-45: Toward educational and social reconstruction

The public concern for the social welfare of young people combined in the closing years of the 1939-45 war with the resolve of Government to lay the foundations of social and educational reconstruction. The unity of post-war reconstruction has been described by Ranson (1994) as a 'political settlement', a contract between the estates of the realm: capital, labour and the state. Various proposals for the development of provision for the continued education, beyond the minimum school leaving age, of young people were brought together and consolidated in the 1944 Education Act.

In 1939, Circular 1486 had been sent from the Board of Education to all LEAs. Its opening paragraph summarised the prevalent concerns:

> The social and physical development of boys and girls between the ages of 14 and 20 who have ceased full-time education has for long been neglected in this country.... War emphasises the defect in our social services: today the blackout, the strain of war and the disorganisation of family life have created conditions which constitute a serious menace to youth. The Government are determined to prevent the recurring, during this war, of the social problems which succeeded the last (para. 1).

The Circular recorded the decision of the Board of Education to take responsibility for youth welfare as part of the national system of education.

The local education authorities were called upon to establish local committees, under the aegis of a National Youth Committee, based upon partnership between the authorities and voluntary bodies in the 'common enterprise' of supporting youth welfare in their areas. These measures were intended to form the foundation of 'an ordered scheme' to serve the needs of youth in the areas of the authorities. Circular 1516 outlined the nature of LEA involvement and stated the purposes of the schemes, which were to promote 'the social and physical training of young people for the responsibilities of citizenship' while Circular 1577 required compulsory registration of all young people aged 16 and 17 with the local authorities, which would offer advice on constructive leisure pursuits and opportunities for voluntary contributions to the war effort in their localities. The latter was a controversial move and one whose success was limited both in terms of the take-up of opportunities for advice, and in increased organisation attachment.

The White Paper on Educational Reconstruction (1943) recommended that provisions which had been developed should not be regarded as a war-time expedient but rather that the basis established should be built upon within the national system of education.

The 1944 Education Act duly made it a duty of authorities, subject to the approval of the Minister, to secure appropriate facilities as part of their educational provision. The 1944 Act was also the vehicle for restatement of the principles of the 1918 Act in respect of the necessity of formal provision for the continued education of young people outside the full-time educational system. The 1944 Act had the clear intention of strengthening the provisions of the 1918 Act by making them compulsory on all parties involved and thereby securing universal part-time day education for all young workers. The provisions of the Act centred on the introduction of a new institution - the County College. County Colleges were to be provided by the local authorities. These were to be

> Centres approved by the Minister for providing for young persons who are not in full-time attendance at any school or other educational institution, such further education, including physical, practical and vocational training, as will enable them to develop their various aptitudes and capacities and will prepare them for the responsibilities of citizenship. (Section 44)

Young persons under 18 years were to be directed to attend a County College for the equivalent of one day a week, and employers were to be directed to release their young employees for the specified times. A timetable for implementation of the plans was drawn up but was almost immediately postponed, the justification being the unavailability of the necessary resources of buildings, manpower and finance. The postponement was an indefinite one, and no succeeding government found itself either willing or able to propose a target date for completion of the programme, the plans for which ultimately became redundant, overtaken by changing circumstances and events.

The proposals of the 1944 Act had attracted wide public discussion. Although the fundamental principle of the responsibility of a society to provide for the continued education of all its young people was generally supported, the purposes of such education for those in employment was a matter surrounded by controversy. Employers' organisations tended, on the whole, to see the purpose of continued education in strictly vocational terms, while the Trades Unions strongly and insistently promoted the view that the central purpose of continued education should be to help young people to lead fuller and happier lives and should, therefore, be directed primarily towards general education.

Many other groups supported the view that education should serve both vocational and non-vocational purposes, claiming that for young people in employment their job was a central concern in their lives, and that post-school education which ignored or failed to relate to it in some way was likely to be regarded as irrelevant by the recipients. This was the view adopted by the Ministry of Education. It was embodied in the 1944 Act and was subsequently expanded and clarified in Pamphlets Nos. 3 and 8, produced for the guidance of local authorities in matters relating, respectively, to the nature of the curriculum which was to be introduced in the proposed County Colleges and to the local organisation of further education. Particular emphasis was placed on the development of close links between the developing youth service provision and the County College programmes.

The post-war years

In the immediate post-war years a massive expansion took place to increase the level of technical skills in the workforce and provision for technical education, geared primarily characterised by formal instruction in evening or part-time day courses in technical colleges. Promotion of organised socially educative activity through the youth service and related forms of provision was slower to take shape.

The growth of technical education

Despite the postponement of implementation of the plans for universal day-time education of the 15-18s, the increasing demand for day release courses, which had begun immediately after the war, continued. The preparations which had been initiated after the Act had stimulated voluntary effort in day release, as had the moves under the concurrent Department of Employment initiatives towards rationalisation and expansion of training provision in industry. The Technical Colleges became full to overflowing with young people who had been released by their employers for further education. The vast majority were released because of their need for vocational education and training. The demand for technical courses designed for those young people in skilled occupations requiring extensive vocational training, therefore, far outweighed the demand for general courses, or for technical courses designed for the semi-skilled or skilled. In addition, substantial numbers of young people to whom release was not available, notably in the commercial and clerical occupations, continued to follow vocational evening courses.

Construction of the Youth Service

The first steps taken in the expansion of 'social education' provision were to clarify the purposes and content of the newly established Youth Service. As in the case of the County College plans, this was an innovative venture which required construction of an adequate conceptual framework in terms both of purposes, strategies and organisation.

The roles and purposes of the service were explained in a series of documents. The 1943 Board of Education Pamphlet, 'The Youth Service after the War', pointed to the main needs which the Youth Service should be attempting to meet. It pinpointed problems of the amount of work demanded of boys and girls both in their jobs and in associated study. It also echoed the concerns voiced in the 1909 Paper, in its observations on the nature and quality of that work, and its potential effects on the developing individuals:

> Young people inevitably spend much of their lives on work which is essential to production, but which does nothing whatever to develop their personalities and may, indeed, positively damage them. Machinery involves monotonous work for many of its servants, and thousands of them are well content ..... with repetitive work; but we must not lose in the machinery the souls of our young men and women. If, as may well be the case, there is no solution to this problem inside working hours, much more urgent is an increase in the amount of a young worker's leisure and the possible use of it to produce, through genuine recreation, the fullest flowering of every side of a developing personality (para. 18).

Although the Youth Service was to cater for all young people beyond the compulsory school leaving age, particular emphasis was placed on those in the less skilled and unskilled occupations with few opportunities for continued education.

Despite the plethora of documents, and the new enthusiasms generated by the 1944 Act, the newly established service was severely under-resourced. It was repeatedly given low priority in the competition for Government funds, on which it became increasingly dependent as the spirit and ethos of voluntarism, fundamental to the 'partnership' principle on which the service was based, began to wane.

The long-term effects were clear. In Jeffs' (1979) words

> The immediate post-war years were to set the seal on a decade-and-a-half of slow, unremitting decline ..... (p. 27)

Given the low priority afforded to broader forms of young worker education, coupled with doubts about the efficacy of the activity-based social education, the only forms of educational provision to flourish were the narrowly technical forms.

The Crowther, Albemarle and Henniker-Heaton Reports

The inadequacy of the existing provisions to meet the educational needs of the age group led to the establishment of the Committees which produced the 'Crowther' and 'Albemarle' Reports in the 1950s. These were two products of the 'great Advisory Councils' whose mission was to remodel educational provision along social democratic lines. Central aims were to foster equality of opportunity, raise expectations and broaden horizons on the basis that equality of opportunity and influence are 'presuppositions' of citizenship. (Ranson, 1994)

The Central Advisory Council was asked, in 1956, to review and report on provisions for the education of 15-18 year olds, in relation to the changing social and industrial conditions and the needs of both society and the individual. The context was economic growth and near full employment, combined with strong moves towards social democratic principles. The findings prompted the formulation of far-reaching recommendations which appeared in the 1959 'Crowther' Report.

Particular attention was paid both to the needs of the 'majority without education' and to those of the young employee in part-time education. Its arguments for provision for the majority were again based on recognition that the processes of learning and development did not come to an end on leaving school.

> For most of them these years (16 to 17) mark the last stages on the long journey from the complete dependence of childhood to the independence of early adult life. Towards its end there is a rapid acceleration in the speed of transition ..... Over most of the environment the educational authorities have no control ..... but we can at least see that some small part of their environment has as its role the concern of seeing that journey is safely accomplished (para. 265).

To discharge both of these responsibilities through the educational system was in the national interest, as well as in the interests of the young people. Expressing its firm view that compulsion must be introduced, firstly on employers to release young people for education, and subsequently on employees to participate, the Committee recommended that a date for compulsory introduction of educational release for all young workers be announced immediately. Its concern to name the date stemmed from a fear that the recommendations would again be shelved: 'one reason why day release has not expanded to take in many semi-skilled and unskilled workers is to be found in the widespread belief that the County College clauses of the Act of 1944 are as dead as the corresponding clauses of the Act of 1918' (para. 283).

The Committee considered that the phased introduction of compulsory attendance at County Colleges should be implemented after the raising of the school leaving age, which it considered to be a first priority. The Committee gave detailed consideration to the type of curriculum which might most appropriately be developed. It suggested the famous 'four strands' as the basis for the curriculum for those students not obtaining or requiring day release for education associated directly with their jobs. The strands were based on the tasks to which the curriculum should be directed:

First, that of helping young workers to find their way successfully about the adult world.

Second, that of helping them to define standards of moral values.

Third, that of helping them to carry over into working life, physical and aesthetic pursuits and activities started at school.

Fourth, that of providing further education in the more formal sense. This element, the Report suggested, should be primarily vocational.

The four strands had some parallels in the curriculum of the German compulsory continuation schools, as these evolved in the 50s and 60s. In Germany, there was a move away from Kerschensteiner's original tenet that trade instruction should form the basis of all teaching, with the scope of teaching extending naturally outwards from the specific practice of the trade and trade skills, towards an understanding of the interdependence of all aspects of life and of all persons in the continuous advancement and welfare of the state. In practice 'civic instruction' had come to be taught as a separate subject, covering such areas as young people in family, work and in public; forms and rules of living together; political information and communities; social questions; German history and 'Germany in the community of races'. Religious instruction, physical education and language teaching also featured strongly in the curriculum.

A significant difference between the German and British approaches was that, in Germany, these strands ran through compulsory vocational training for all, and were seen as essential preparation for work. The distinction between *essential* education and training for skilled occupations and socially desirable education for 'the rest' was not drawn in the way it was in England, since most young people were actively encouraged to work towards skilled occupations of one kind or another. 'Apprenticeship' was much broader in scope and covered many more occupational fields than the British equivalent. It was not 'age-tied' and by providing opportunities to enter apprenticeships in the late teens and beyond there were incentives for those initially unsuccessful to continue in their efforts to gain and complete an apprenticeship. The exception to this was in the domestic 'training' provided for young women through the domestic vocational schools. Training for the roles of wife and mother was presented as crucially important in the national interest (another of Kerschensteiner's central tenets). In practice the training in the domestic schools was generally of a low standard and much more narrowly drawn than the training provided in the commercial and industrial vocational schools.

In Britain, the Crowther Report questioned the efficacy of both further education and the Youth Service in 'attracting and serving' young people who had left school at the earliest opportunity, and providing the necessary 'help in growing up'.

It seems clear, then, that the majority of boys and nearly all girls who leave school as soon as they are legally entitled to do so are without that help in growing up which is acknowledged to be necessary. They do not get day release, nor are they enrolled with the other forms of part-time education that we have considered. How far does the Youth Service provide for their needs? Or does it, on the contrary, mainly attract and serve only those who also enjoy the assistance of other educational agencies? (p. 261)

Summarising its evaluation of both the formal and non-formal forms of provision, Crowther said:

It is unfortunately ...... clear that, for boys in the semi-skilled and unskilled occupations, and for almost all girls, the present provision is unsatisfactory and without visible promise of improvement. Those who most need support in the critical years of adolescence get least. This is true both of part-time education and the Youth Service. (p. 263)

The Crowther Committee saw a strong Youth Service as an essential complement to the County Colleges and recommended that steps be taken to develop it during the period of preparation for the implementation of the County College plans.

The decline of the post-war years which had left the Youth Service 'dying on its feet' led, in the face of growing demands for action, to the establishment of the Albemarle Committee, whose 1960 Report was to provide an intellectual identity for the Youth Service and the basis for a decade of expansion. The developmental needs of young people entering work at the earliest school leaving ages again provoked special comment:

We are particularly conscious of the lack of opportunity which, in the absence of the County Colleges, industry in general provides for many working girls or for many boys to have continued educational experience or to develop their personality at work. It is to young people such as these that society owes a special debt, since they leave the educational system earlier than many of their contemporaries. This debt can be paid in part by a Youth Service which can provide adequately for their development as adults and citizens (para. 112).

Drawing attention to the 'comparative poverty' of the provision for social development available to those entering working life, in comparison with that available to those continuing in secondary and higher education, the Report observed that:

If these informal activities are needed by 15 year olds today, they will be needed by 16 year olds tomorrow; if they are needed by those up to 21 years of age today (so long as they are in full-time education), they are undoubtedly needed by all those whose intellectual equipment has not been sufficient to keep them under the comfortable umbrella of full-time education (para. 131).

The service envisaged by Albemarle was primarily social and pastoral in nature, and closely integrated with further education. Its main elements, it suggested, should be association, training and challenge, with the age limit returned to 14-20. The importance of a bridging period between school and work was the underlying argument for this recommendation.

The recommendations of the Albemarle Report for a 10 year development programme, aimed at the expansion of the Youth Service and its alignment with Further Education, were accepted by the Minister of Education, and subsequently implemented in a programme which involved doubling the spending of local authorities on youth work. Citizenship education was seen as part of good youth work practice:

> Playing one's part as a citizen is highly important, and the activities of the Youth Service are relevant to it. But the beginnings of 'citizenship' can be seen as much in the subtlety and tact of social relations in a good youth club, even in a tough area, as in straight-forward discussions of good citizenship (para. 144).

The 1960s were, therefore, a time of growth and expansion for the Youth Service. The 60s also saw a movement towards liberalisation of technical education, an extension of opportunities for part-time day education for those in commercial and clerical occupations, under the influences of the major educational reports of the period, and the White Papers on Technical Education of 1956 and 1961, while questions of the practicalities of extending educational release were again investigated, following the Crowther recommendations, culminating in the Henniker-Heaton Report of 1964.

The Committee, set up under the chairmanship of C Henniker-Heaton, had, as its terms of reference:

> To report on what steps should be taken to bring about the maximum practicable increases in the granting of release from employment to enable young persons under the age of 18 to attend technical and other courses of Further Education.

Consultations prior to the establishment of the Committee, involving a range of educational and industrial interests, had produced unanimous agreement that there was 'a serious numerical shortfall' in educational release in industry and commerce which ought to be remedied. It had, simultaneously, produced agreement that neither compulsion in day release nor the right to claim release could be granted at that time without holding back the prospects of other urgent educational developments, including the expansion of Higher Education The Committee was empowered, therefore, only to look at ways in which increases in the amount of day release granted might be achieved within the existing voluntary system and within strictly limited resources. Its recommendations were correspondingly circumscribed and the Report was overshadowed by the passing of the Industrial Training Act in the same year. This Act was regarded by many educationalists as presenting the best hope for extension of educational opportunity for young people in employment, for some time.

The training revolution

Under the terms of the Act, educational interests were to have substantial representation on the new Industrial Training Boards, and a requirement of the Act in respect of further education was that the Boards should recommend which courses of further education were appropriately pursued in association with industrial training. While the Act described neither the nature of the relationship between training and associated further education, nor the issue of which trainees should receive educational release, these two areas were dealt with subsequently. While the Act was welcomed by some in the education services as a potential instrument for expansion, many were disturbed by the reinforcement of a system of education and training in which the finance and responsibility for the two components was divided. There was particular concern that the new system would place the initiative for further education with industry, rather than with the education services, thus preserving the essence of voluntarism and perpetuating the role of further education as the 'handmaiden of industry' with all that implied for curricular aims and purposes.

The implementation of the Act, combined with the recommendations of the Henniker-Heaton Report, was expected to produce a rapid expansion in educational release in the late 60s and 70s. The colleges, in many cases, prepared themselves for a substantially increased intake. The trends in release were, in actuality, quite different from those predicted. Between 1966 and 1976 the numbers released in England and Wales in the 16-18 age group decreased from 366,861 to 249,534. In the 19-20 age group the numbers decreased from 144,572 to 124,932 between 1966 and 1976. The sharp decrease can be attributed to number of factors. These include the trends in the number of young people in employment, the continuing reluctance of employers to release young employees for courses whose benefits to the employer are relatively intangible and the streamlining of apprentice intake in the process of training rationalisation.

The decline was, nevertheless, a blow to those who, perhaps by misinterpretation of the nature and intentions of the Act, had seized on it as a means to extend the scope and extent of further education, in some cases in directions which had little demonstrable relevance to employers' primary needs.

Bury of the Confederation of British Industry, speaking in 1972 to the Association of Colleges of Further and Higher Education said that:

> ..... Education in the general sense of the term is not, and cannot be, industry's first priority .....

Venables commented on the way in which the outcomes of the Act had revealed the 'absurdity of relying on that reified entity 'Industry' to provide education, as distinct from training, for the large proportion of young people who leave school at 16' (p.14). She welcomed what she saw as the end of paternalism in industry and looked for the Government's recognition that the social necessity of the provision of educational opportunity was 'too important to be left to the whims of employers'. It served to demonstrate, again, the conflicts in respect of educational goals and priorities inherent in a system characterised by voluntarism and by dual responsibility for education and training. The German dual system of VET, by contrast, had been underpinned by both legislation and social consensus, buttressed by notions of common purpose on both sides of industry - employers and trades unions. Corporatist strands were particularly strong in Germany, and West Germany was 'exceptional in the harmony displayed by the leading economic groups and evident at all levels' (Smith, 1982). Calls for immediate strengthening and extension of legislation along German lines often missed this point of essential difference between the German and British socio-cultural contexts.

Developments of the 1970s

Meanwhile, the whole educational context within which the debate on the educational participation of young people at work was located, was changing as rapidly as the industrial context. The decision to raise the school leaving age, with effect from 1972/73, extended full-time education to all 15 year olds. Changes in the relationships between education and work were producing an unprecedented situation in 16-19 education, within which traditional education aims and functions and their associated organisational and curriculum practices were being questioned. Edmund King, in the first major study of post-compulsory education in a comparative Western European context, found that the effects of combined contextual, structural and conceptual change had produced an urgent need to develop polyvalent education for the 16-19s, characterised by participative teaching and learning strategies, and geared to expectations of autonomous responsibility for their own learning beyond the adolescent phase. This needed to be done by emphasising 'operational', rather than 'cumulative' aims in education and by developing both personal and vocational aptitudes necessary to meet the uncertainties of the future (King, 1974).

New directions in vocational preparation

In the early 1970s attention was focused sharply on meeting the rapidly expanding demand for full-time post-compulsory education. The problems of discontinuity and broken transitions from education to employment, which were to become the preoccupation of the 1980s, were only just beginning to emerge. Despite these developments elsewhere in the system, the continuing decline of educational release and the continuing failure of the Youth Services to attract greater participation among young adults in general, and among young adults in employment in particular, had brought the issue of provision for universal and compulsory post-school day education once more to the forefront. It seemed that voluntarism in all its forms had failed and that such advances as had been achieved were slowly being eroded. Accordingly, the 1970s saw a proliferation of papers and statements again advocating Government action to secure improved opportunities for young people at work.

The Labour Party, City and Guilds of London Institute, and the National Association of Teachers in Further and Higher Education, all published documents urging early and effective action, citing both social justice and economic arguments for improved education for young workers. There were signs, however, that fresh thinking was emerging within the educational and training sectors about the appropriateness of existing modes of post-school education available to those in employment, particularly for those in the semi-skilled and unskilled occupations. The issues of quality and effectiveness raised by the Crowther and Albemarle Committees, and submerged in the waves of enthusiasm for expansion, were rising again to the surface. In educational terms, the wisdom of determining the mode of study ('day release') in advance of questions of learning needs and motivations was open to serious question. The need for fundamental reassessment of existing modes, and consideration of possible alternatives, was beginning to be expressed. One of the main stumbling-blocks was seen to be the artificial separation of education from experience, which removes education to a context remote from those elements of learning which are perceived by young people as being of immediate and direct benefit to them, and which are, in many cases, the principal motivating factors.
Facing the facts of poor motivation towards education among many of those whose interests were meant to be served by it, consideration began to be given to alternative models which draw together education, training and

experience in one complete programme, by a number of providing agencies.

Thinking along these lines was already being developed elsewhere. Since its inception, substantial advances had been made by the Manpower Services Commission in reviewing the training and educational opportunities of young people entering employment, and in developing new schemes. The work of a Joint Working Party of the Department of Employment and Department of Education and Science, convened in the early 1970s to consider the possible responses to the contemporary needs of young adults, for the first time drew together the issues surrounding the extent and quality of further education and its relationship with training, as a basis for action.

In 1976 a programme of pilot schemes was launched which attempted to provide unified education, training and experience for those in employment who were receiving little or no opportunity for further education. The programme was designed to assess alternative forms of provision which would attract young people, meet their wider needs, and win employers' support, recognising that the existing further education models, while reasonably successful with the traditional participants, were clearly inappropriate when transferred to the non-participant majority. The aims of the programme were to assist young people:

i. To assess their potential and think realistically about jobs and careers;
ii. To develop the basic skills which will be needed in adult life generally;
iii. To understand their society and how it works;
iv. To strengthen the foundation of skill and knowledge on which further training and education can be built.

The programme, clearly designed to support young people in the achievement of major 'growth tasks' extending beyond the strictly vocational, was termed a programme of 'Unified Vocational Preparation', heralding the development of a new concept of preparation for adult and working life which was to become of growing significance.

While the emphasis was primarily 'vocational' in terms of presentation and description of the activities, the notion of the social development of young people was clearly in evidence. The development of a vocational 'presentation' was deemed essential in a form of provision which relies on the voluntary participation of employers and requires release from employment, or at least material support. The wider educational aspects were embodied as adjuncts in such developments and integrated with the directly vocational aspects. Here they were less susceptible to rejection than they are in separate provision which distinguishes between education and training, but subject to the pitfalls of making citizenship an adjunct, as outlined in the opening chapter.

Re-orientation of the Youth Services

The Youth Services during this period, too, saw the emergence of challenges to the traditionally established modes and approaches. The advances made after Albemarle, it seemed, had made little impact on the target and age group in question. The Fairbairn and Milson Committees, meeting under the Youth Service Development Council to review the progress of the Youth Services in the post-Albemarle period, identified some particular problems and obstacles to the effective meeting of needs of young adults, particularly those in employment. These were the juvenile image of the Service, its frequent failure to offer real responsibility to its older participants and, more fundamentally, its very nature, segregating the social activity of young people from the adult society into which they seek to be integrated.

The aims of both 'arms' of the Service, statutory and voluntary had, since their inception, been concerned principally with the inculcation into young people of the 'universalistic' norms of society through age segregated provision. The aims, propounded in the 1969 Report, represented a radical departure in their notions of the preparation of young adults for 'critical involvement' in the 'active society'. They were, however, to have little long-term impact on the direction of structure of the services for youth. They were rejected by the Minister of Education in 1971 on the grounds that there was insufficient evidence that the approaches advocated reflected the felt needs or demands of young people in reality. It was recommended that the traditional forms of activity and organisation continue to be the basis for provision across the whole age range of the Service. Nevertheless, the Report did stimulate new thinking in Youth Service personnel at all levels, and the community debate has continued. There can be few issues so much reviewed over such a long period of time with so little action resulting.

Even in the strong social democratic programme of the 60s and 70s, the recognised wastage of the potential and latent abilities of young people who entered the labour market early, without access to education and training, was in the last analysis considered affordable, if undesirable, when priorities for resource allocation had to be decided.

When the focus shifted from 'wastage of talent' to 'economic competitiveness' and, less explicitly, to the threat posed by growing numbers of marginalised and excluded young people, the picture changed dramatically.

3 Gaining the competitive edge?

> As I saw them, the purposes of the Review were to ..... support the achievement of the new National Targets for Education and Training, with their aim of providing a national workforce able to meet the international competitive challenge through high levels of skill and adaptability to change.

Sir Ron Dearing, March 1996

The international context has come to dominate policy reviews of post-compulsory education and training. There is much talk of Asian Tigers and of Skills Revolutions. Competitiveness has become the mantra of the approach to the millennium with education presented as crucial to this elusive goal.

Sir Geoffrey Crowther, the 1950s counterpart of Sir Ron Dearing, opened his report with the words 'This report is about the education of English boys and girls aged between fifteen and eighteen. Most of them are not being educated'. The most marked contrast with the Dearing Reports of the 1990s is that most are being educated, in one way or another.

The percentage of young people continuing their education after 16 has tripled since the 1950s and the proportion entering Higher Education has increased from less than 1 in 20 to current levels of almost 1 in 3.

Figure 3.1 shows the percentage of 16 year olds staying on in full-time education increasing to over 70 per cent, with study for Advanced (A) Levels predominant and the wedges at the end representing growth of General National Vocational Qualifications (GNVQs). But this is only part of the picture.

Figure 3.2 shows the system as envisaged by the National Council for Vocational Qualifications, with the academic degree, which historically dominated the system, dwarfed by an emerging edifice of national vocational qualifications (NVQs and GNVQs). This essentially divided structure, known as the *triple track*, was initially preserved by Dearing's proposals for 16-19 qualifications (Dearing 1996), the differences being the renaming of GNVQ level 3 (half-way up the middle column) as Applied A levels, with opportunities to achieve a common National Award via each track, subject to criteria of breadth and depth being met. Crowther, in reviewing the problem of what he termed the 'majority without education' in the late 50s, was grappling with the legacies of the tripartite system of schooling put in place through the 1994 (Butler) Education Act, which established Grammar schools, Technical Schools and Secondary Moderns.

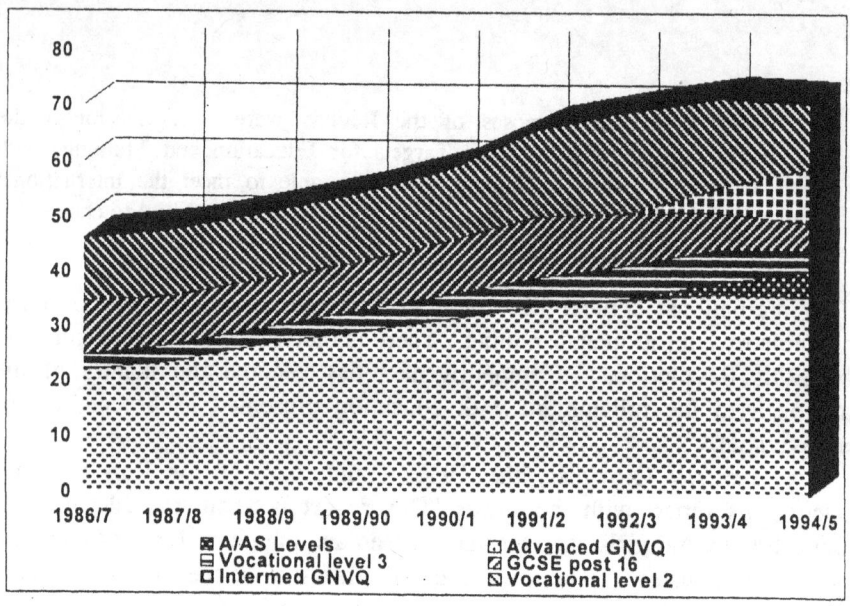

Figure 3.1: Full-time participation by course at 16: percentage of cohort increasing to over 70 percent by mid-90s

This triple track education of the 1940s was presented as offering forms of education which were different but equal in esteem, with selection at 11 to ensure that young people were directed to the form of education most suited to their particular talents and abilities. In practice the Secondary Moderns, the brave new invention of the 1944 act, far from being equal but different, were inevitably held in low esteem, producing what Brown and Lauder (1992) have termed 'trained incapacity' in a significant proportion of the population. The issue rapidly became one of wastage of talent and potential through premature selection, and much evidence was produced of the extent of untapped, unrecognised ability, and where it lay. It lay in able young

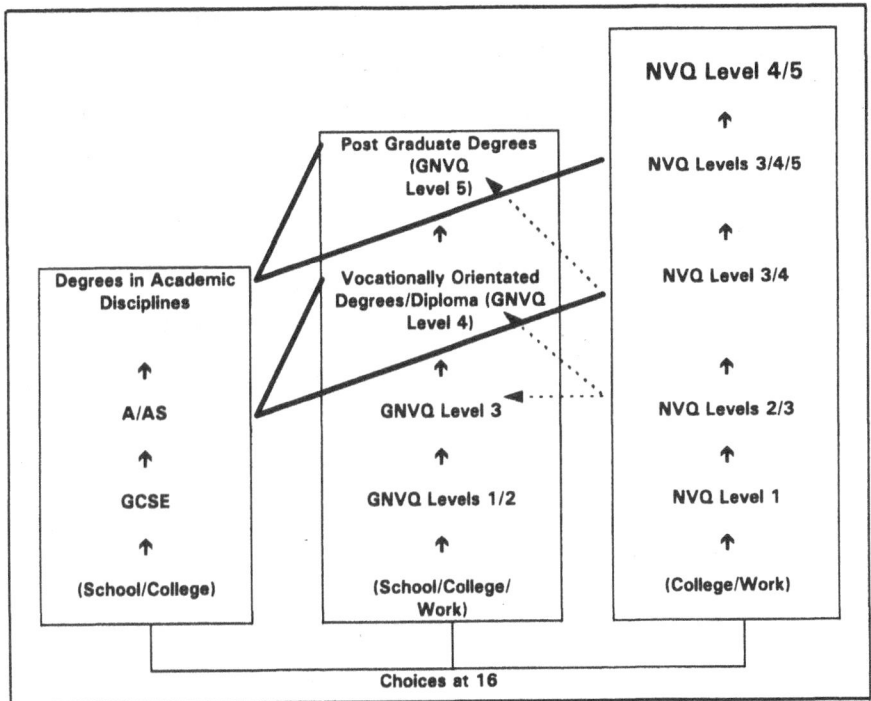

Figure 3.2: The triple track model of post-16 qualifications, NCVQ

people from working class backgrounds, as Douglas, Ross and Simpson (1968) showed. Tracing the progress of over five thousand children born in 1946, they demonstrated the extent of under-achievement among working class children by providing evidence of the differences in attainment of good certificates among young people who had equal inherent ability, but different social class backgrounds. The wastage of talent that also lay in the female half of the population was less readily recognised, despite evidence that girls performed better academically than boys up to 16 but were cooled out and spiralled down by the system after that, while Newsom's report 'Half our Future' perpetuated the view that 'many, perhaps most' girls regarded marriage as their 'most important vocational concern' (Ministry of Education 1963).

The previous chapter showed how Crowther's recommendations emphasised the need to remedy the lack of opportunity for the 'majority without education' with an implicit emphasis on working class males, but his proposals that immediate steps should be taken to implement universal access of all young workers to receive broad-based part-time education, through County Colleges, were too expensive and in competition with his own and the subsequent recommendations of the Robbins Committee to expand access to Higher Education. With an eye on the middle class voters, the Robbins recommendations of 1963 were given priority, with ten institutions immediately upgraded to University status and a further six new universities created towards the aim of enabling all those qualified and deemed able to benefit to have access to Higher Education.

In the midst of the competing policy priorities of the 60s and 70s, relatively little was done about the majority who left school at the earliest opportunity and went straight into the labour market. It is important to remember that this was then the normal experience of young people, with more than 70 per cent going straight into jobs at 16.

As unemployment increased in the 80s, it was this group of young adults who were most affected by the collapse in apprenticeship in the recession and those entering the labour market without qualifications or significant skills to offer were in an even worse plight. It was in this decade of unemployment and economic decline that the three key words associated with Thatcherism came to the fore in policies for education and training:

- **enterprise** - **flexibility** - **competitiveness**.

Lack of these qualities explained Britain's economic decline, it was said, with education identified as both the cause and solution. All this was initially set in train by the famous Ruskin speech of James Callaghan (1976), which said education was not instrumental enough in producing qualities employers need, and set the scene for a new wave of policies, including the rushed introduction of youth training schemes as short term remedies to the politically embarrassing problem of unemployed young people on the streets. By 1986 Youth Training Schemes had doubled in length and tripled in take up as the labour market was unable to absorb school leavers, who together with the schools continued to be blamed for their predicament. They did not have jobs because they did not have the right skills and attributes, and schools and colleges had failed both society and young people by failing to equip them adequately, it was said.

Education and work were seen as separate and mutually exclusive domains, the old dualism, with one part (education) failing the other (industry and commerce). Something had to be done, and with an approach akin to the 'four legs good, two legs bad' of the Animal Farm, the then Manpower Services Commission promulgated the belief that 'work-driven approaches were good, education-driven bad' leading inevitably to the conclusion that in bringing education and work together, education should become subordinate to and itself driven by the values and standards of work. Concepts of competence thus came to dominate the debate about what should be done about education after sixteen, and the triple track came into being.

In the ensuing debate between those who reject a purely instrumental role for education and those who have little time for what they see as the wider and self serving aims of the educational community, core skills came to the fore. These appeared, superficially at least, to offer a means of describing the general attributes required in and for work, in ways which could be identified with and subscribed to by both employers and teachers.

Pressures for a core curriculum for youth work also emerged, instigated by the government in pursuit of measurable outcomes and performance indicators comparable with other branches of the educational services.

How far were the policies successful in achieving their goals?

There are three levels to be considered here: **policy as espoused, policy as enacted, policy as experienced.**

Policy as espoused centres on the National Education and Training Targets (NETT) Much work has gone into statistical projections about these. The Foundation Level 3 target (2 A levels or vocational equivalent) was that 60 per cent of young people should be achieving this level by the year 2000. Contributions of the three tracks to this target at the time of the Dearing review are shown in a pie chart, Fig 3.3, based on counting methods used by Institute of Education and University of Warwick.

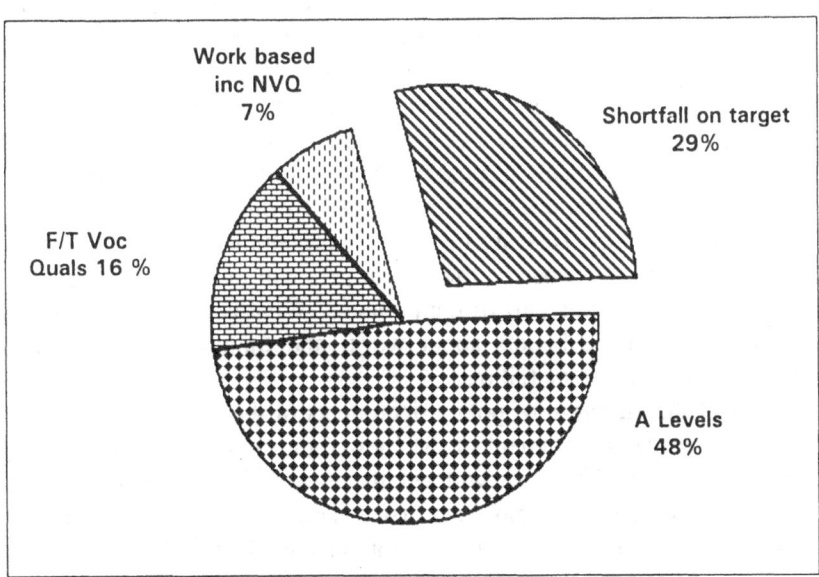

Figure 3.3: Foundation 3 Target - Progress at 1996

The academic Advanced Level track was making the biggest contribution to the target, with currently close to half coming from A levels. 16 per cent came from full-time Vocational Qualifications in which growth has been concentrated since 1991, and only 7 per cent from the work-based route, leaving a 29 per cent shortfall to be made up by 2000. The key issue was the growth which could be expected, and whether the target was within reach.

Little further growth was expected from the academic A level source, possibly even a reduction given the Dearing proposals to make A level 'harder'.

The low figures in full-time vocational qualifications reflected poor completion rates, with only slightly more than half of students completing Advanced GNVQs successfully even after additional time, compared with successful completion rates of more than 70 per cent in traditional vocational qualifications such as the Business and Technician Education Council (BTEC) Diploma. There was real potential for growth if improvements associated with their renaming as 'Applied A levels' could achieve significant increases in completion rates. Additionally, the number achieving Level 3 via the work-based route was still small, reflecting generally low take up and completion of NVQs. Renewed plans to boost this route by 2000 through Modern Apprenticeships showed a continuing belief in the ability of voluntary employer-led schemes to deliver major programmes, despite their long and sustained history of failure in doing so.

In opposition to Dearing, the National Commission on Education (1973), sponsored by the British Academy and chaired by Lord Walton, drew attention to the mounting evidence that the pre-eminence of the academic A level and the single minded devotion to keeping it intact as an élite qualification, had not only cast a shadow over vocational and applied studies, but had also made it possible for young people to follow the narrowest post-16 curriculum in the developed world. While breadth may have been tackled by the Dearing review, the pre-eminence of the academic A level has not, and the progress towards targets will inevitably reflect that.

But targets are only one part of the policies. What is more important, in many ways, is people's beliefs about work, and training, and individual responsibility for success or failure.

Analysis of the language of policy documents of the 80s and 90s reveals the reality which the government of the 'new right' aimed to construct: that individual effort and enterprise will get its rewards in the labour market, and if they do not come we have not tried hard enough for long enough, we have not been flexible enough or 'got on our bikes' when necessary. Much of this stemmed from a fear that a generation would lose the will to work, faced with massive and enduring unemployment, and worse still, would come to blame the government for their plight and take to the streets, as indeed they did, not only in Toxteth and Brixton, but also in Oxford and Bristol. Have the policies worked in these terms? Have they worked attitudinally? Findings from the 16-19 Initiative showed that at the end of the 1980s the level of work commitment amongst those with low skills and experience of unemployment was at least as great as those aiming for highly skilled occupations. There was little evidence there of the work-alienated attitudes of the supposed emerging underclass, a finding also reinforced by MacDonald and Coffield's (1991) study of youth in Teeside.

Scores on attitude items showing how far young people saw themselves as being in control of their own destinies are also of interest, particularly when compared with those of young adults socialised in a version of the American Dream and the myth that anyone can make it to the top through effort and belief in themselves (Fig 3.4). Young Britons were only slightly less prepared to see themselves as personally responsible for their fates than their North American counterparts although they were rather less ready to blame the poor for their state of poverty. Females were more 'internal' in their economic locus of control then males, who tended to be slightly more fatalistic in both countries. However, they showed less motivation to train for jobs involving new technology in both countries (Evans and Taylor, 1997).

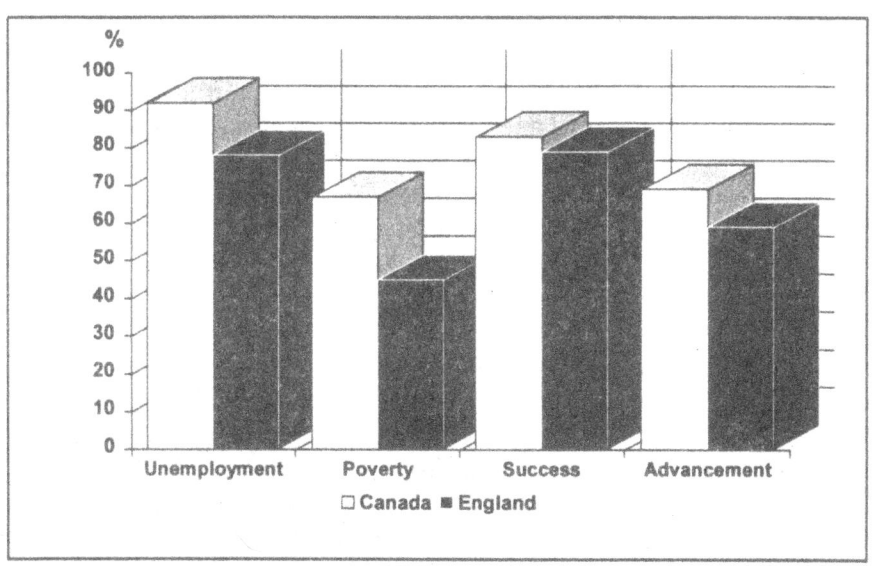

Figure 3.4: Perceptions of individual responsibility for social well-being and career advancement

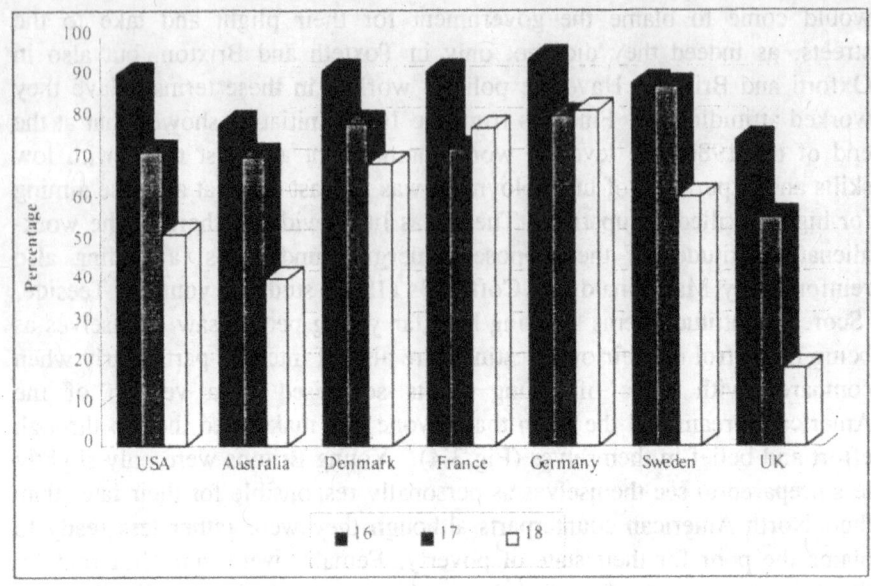

Figure 3.5: Full-time participation in Further Education or equivalent at 16, 17 and 18

In a 1995/96 study of an East London labour market only (Rudd 1996) 18 per cent of young people thought that success or otherwise was determined principally by the features of the job market. As one 18 year old put it, "it's about the effort you put in and the confidence you have in yourself". Many of these students would previously have left education and would have found themselves on what they termed 'govvy schemes', where such beliefs in individual effort declined rapidly with repeated, frustrated attempts to gain a foothold in long term skilled work. Overall, the evidence suggests that retention in education is sustaining belief in individual responsibility and employment confidence, in the short term at least.

In summary, the policies appeared to be working attitudinally, in sustaining *employment confidence* and belief in *individual responsibility*. They have also worked in delivering expansion of numbers *participating*, but *achievement targets* are not being met.

It might be argued that this is just a case of setting ambitious targets to move progress and challenge the system, that real growth has been achieved and can be built on. But targets could not have been set lower given the link with international competitiveness as an aim.

Comparative successes or failures: have the policies worked when compared internationally?

International statistics from the Organisation for Economic Co-operation and Development (OECD) in 1995 (Figure 3.5) showed the relative position of Britain, in sub-degree full-time educational participation. While participation has increased above the levels shown since these data were collected, what has not changed is the relative position and dramatic fall off at the ages of 17 and 18. Even with part-time studies included Britain is still lagging.

The only level at which qualification rates are comparatively good is Higher Education and the expansion of Higher Education combined with relatively good completion rates at this level mean that Britain is likely to maintain its position in the short term at least, although many other countries are also embarked on expansion programmes in Higher Education with OECD predicting that we will see moves to 50 per cent participation rates in many of the advanced economies early in the 21st Century.

So far the discussion has centred on quantitative measures of achievement and participation. But the mere comparison of rates ignores the significance of social and cultural differences. These are highlighted in the comparative research carried out by the author on the experiences of young adults in four cities in England and Germany over a decade.

The rationale for studying Germany goes beyond recognition of the leading role of German thinking and ideals in the sphere of vocational education and training. There is a deep historical affinity between England and Germany which leads Britain to evaluate its progress by looking in that direction. There is a shared history of mediaeval guilds from which an apprenticeship tradition evolved in both countries. In Germany, this tradition, when overlaid with German bureaucracy, developed into the huge institutionalised national system of apprenticeship which covers all occupational fields and absorbs half of school leavers. In Britain, the apprenticeship tradition when overlaid with laissez faire economic liberalism all but disappeared, with regular calls for its return in one form or another whenever things go wrong in British vocational education and training.

Some differences between English and German routes into work

1. Accelerated (E) v. Extended (G) transitions: E more than 2 years ahead in labour market entry in all career tracks;
2. G: emphasis on general labour market utility of apprenticeship qualifications (followed by more than half of all school leavers).
3. G: surrounds young adults with strong institutional structures for education and training, at all levels, into 20s.
   E: non-institutionalised by comparison and surrounds young people with job and work-related substitutes for education.
4. E: higher exposure to 'real' work experiences and responsibilities at earlier stage at all levels.

The difference in age of first labour market entry is most marked at graduate level, where the average age of first entry to the labour market is 28 in Germany compared with 22 in Britain. The higher exposure to 'real' work experiences and responsibilities at an earlier stage at all levels is indicated by the findings shown in Figure 3.6 which compare reported frequency of exposure to different kinds of experiences among young people matched by age, gender and occupational area.

In all categories, English young people in education and training recorded greater frequency of these experiences than their German peers.

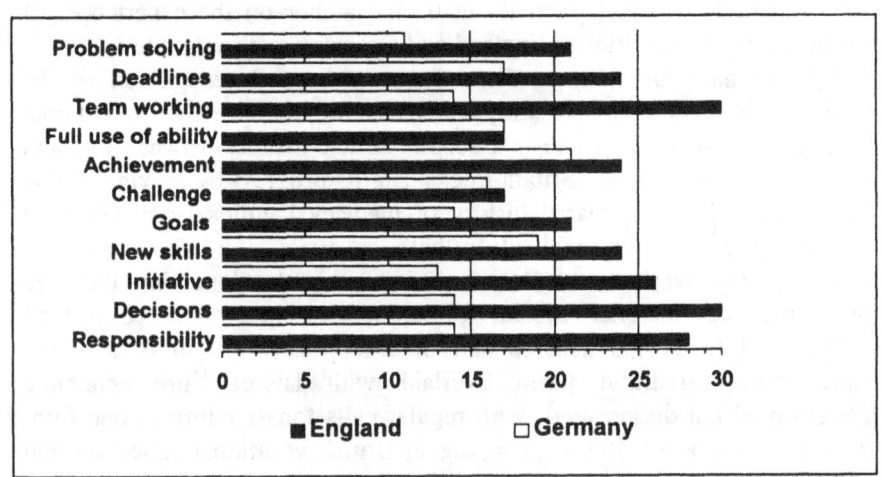

Figure 3.6: General work skills: 16-20 year olds in England (n=320) and Germany (n=320)

Young people were also asked about experience of testing and assessment. Given the image of the rigour of German vocational education, a heavy emphasis on skills testing and examinations might be expected in Germany. In fact, Germans also reported much lower frequency of written and practical tests. Whatever it is that is so successful about the German VET system it appears not to rely on extensive testing and assessment of work-related tasks.

Does the key to German success lie in attitudes? How do young Germans, aged from 16 to early 20s, differ from their English counterparts in attitudes to work and the wider world?

Figure 3.7 shows that young Germans generally scored higher than their English peers on a measure of work commitment. This applied for both males and females and across all skills levels, from skilled to unskilled, in matched samples:

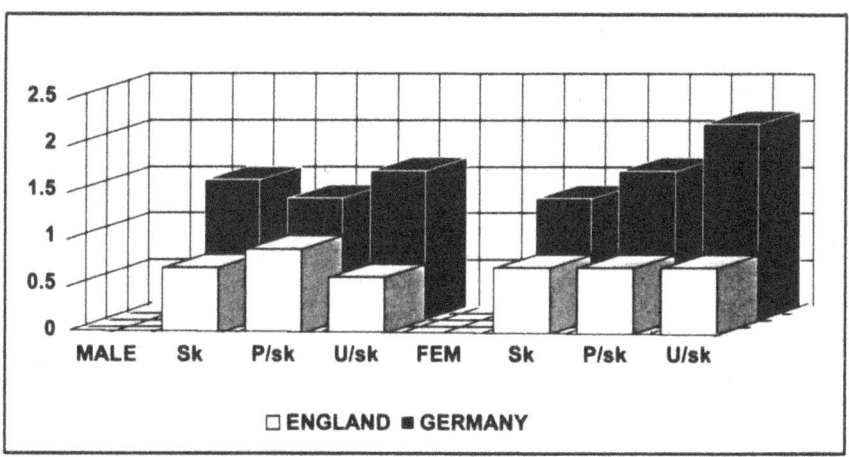

Figure 3.7: Work commitment: 16-20 year olds in England (n=320) and Germany (n=320)

Political interest was also generally higher in Germany. Greater interest in political participation and political issues was found in most groups (Figure 3.8). The Berufsschule in Germany continue to have citizenship and political education as part of their curriculum, first pioneered by Kerschensteiner in 1900. Twentieth Century German history has ensured these elements their place in the post-16 curriculum into the 21st Century although the dangers of 'citizenship' education itself becoming harnessed to nationalistic and propagandist aims were starkly shown in Germany under the Nazis (Smith, 1982; Stradling, 1983). The contrast with Britain is marked in that these elements are practically non-existent in the institutional post-16 curriculum. They are most apparent in youth work, which was encouraged in these aims by the 1982 Thompson Report, only to be later discouraged by the government in the 1991 Review of the youth service. This attempted to identify an outcomes-based 'core curriculum' for the

Youth Service emphasising the role of youth work in containing some of the problems of marginalised youth and downplaying the political and citizenship education aspects.

The only attitude measure which showed the opposite pattern with relatively higher scores in the English samples was, ironically, employment confidence, with greater confidence in all career routes in ability to find and maintain a job in England, although actual prospects of doing so were lower than in Germany (Figure 3.9). Confidence was at its highest in lowest career routes; those least likely to secure stable employment displayed greatest confidence.

This may be more evidence of British policies working in sustaining beliefs; it is, perhaps, also to do with lack of political education, and with the deregulated labour market. Getting a job which comes up by luck is much less likely in Germany. In Liverpool young people were kept going by the belief that something might be just around the corner, even for the least qualified.

So while the work ethic has not been eroded in Britain, and may have been sustained by vocationalism in education, culturally it is at much lower levels than in Germany, with whom traditionally comparisons have been made.

Significantly more Germans than English expected to obtain further qualifications after starting work; while more English young people expected to have to retrain for a different job and to have to move to find work. Unsurprisingly, many more Germans expected to learn a new language in adult life than their English counterparts!

Young Germans therefore generally saw their future as building up educational capital within their chosen occupation. For the English, it was more a case of doing what was necessary to get and keep a job. If short termism is the British disease, then these young people were certainly reflecting it (Figure 3.10).

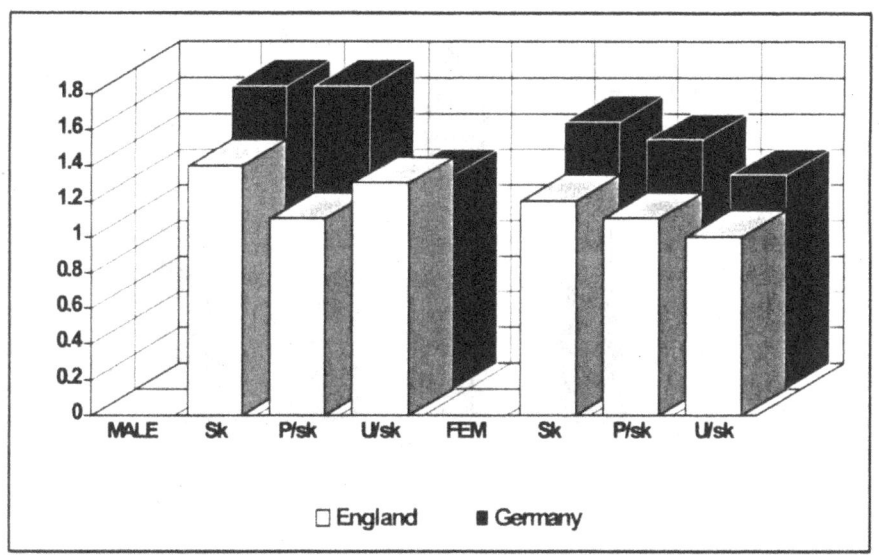

Figure 3.8: Political interest: 16-20 year olds in England (n=320) and Germany (n=320)

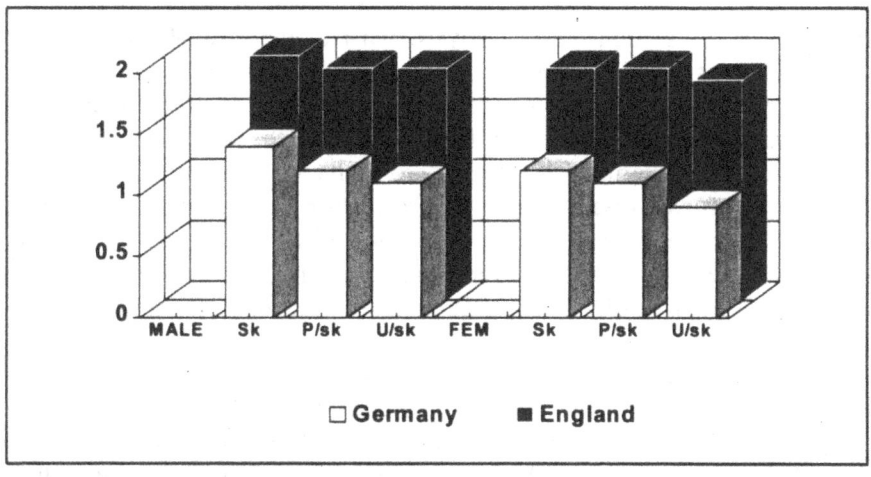

Figure 3.9: Employment confidence: 16-20 year olds in England (n=320) and Germany (n=320)

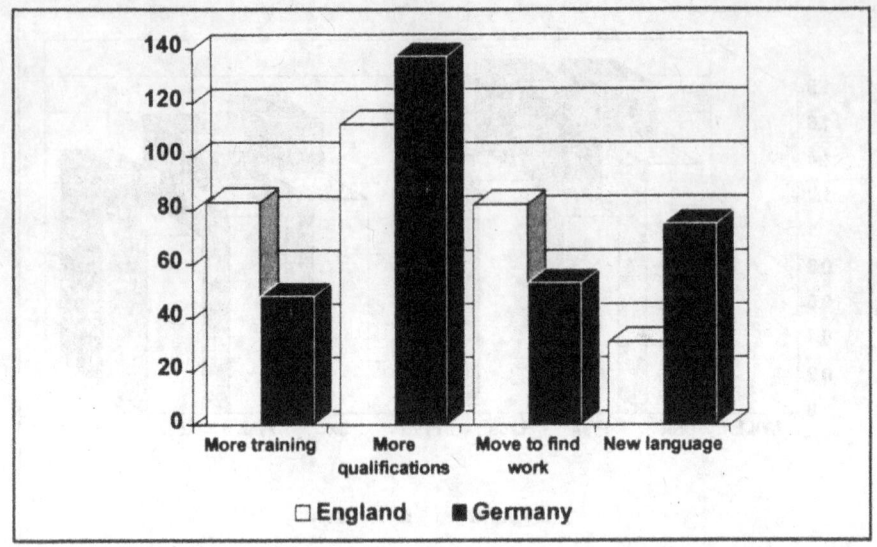

Figure 3.10: Employment expectations: 16-20 year olds in England (n=160) and Germany (n=160)

Finally, for this section of the analysis, what of the goal of international competitiveness itself? Germany is far from trouble free. Its divided system of education is also now producing lack of esteem for vocational studies as more go into Higher Education, and the German vocational routes are more deterministic, with a worse record than Britain in social mobility and gender disadvantage. In the former East, young people have not been socialised to cope with competition in education and the labour market, and recent evidence emerging from ongoing Anglo-German Studies (Evans and Kaluza, 1997) suggests various 'reactions of alienation' are occurring.

Looking over the last 20 years of British policy and the governmental explanations of economic decline, the inadequacies of education and training have been a strong theme. Instead of addressing economic decline through investment in the science base and advanced technological skills, Britain's strategy has rested heavily on removal of perceived barriers to market forces and deregulation of the labour market, in the name of competitiveness.

What are the effects of this? Professor Arthur Francis, Director of the ESRC study on Competitiveness has echoed Paul Krugman[1] in questioning

---

[1] Economist, Massachussetts Institute of Technology, who has argued that the current obsession with competitiveness is 'not only wrong, but dangerous' Krugman (1994)

whether the pursuit of *competitiveness* makes sense as general aim of public policy, arguing that much of the competitiveness problem stems from poor industrial management practices and cannot sensibly be blamed on anti-industrial cultures in the Universities, or short termism in the City nor on poor teaching in schools. Moreover, he finds little evidence of improved competitiveness from the policies in operation since 1979.

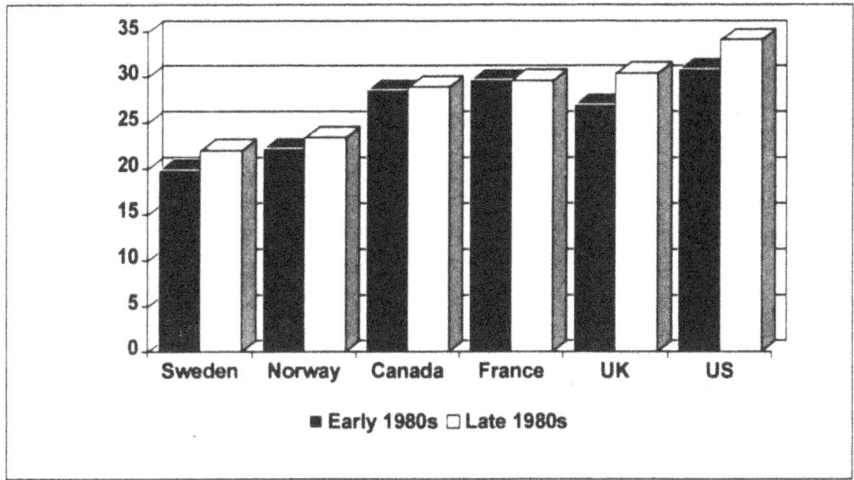

Figure 3.11: Inequality Trend: Changes in GINI co-efficient

Figure 3.11, based on OECD statistics, reveals other effects of the policies and shows that while the United States is the most unequal nation in the developed world, Britain is now close behind with dramatic changes in the 1980s. In 1997, the legal human rights group Justice, in evidence to the UN, showed that the divide between highest-paid and lowest-paid workers was the greatest since 1886. Many of the advanced industrial nations have seen a rise in inequality, explained by collapse in demand for unskilled labour (driving down wages and increasing unemployment); but the steepness of the rise in Britain shows other factors at work, including the effects of high levels of deregulation and casualisation of labour force.

There is evidence of competitiveness pursued through deregulation rather than investment in the science and technology base; evidence of increased social inequality, but little evidence of the increased competitiveness sought.

Comparatively, the policies have produced a mixed picture of success and failure. While Britain is catching up in participation levels, achievement levels are lagging at below-degree level. Competitiveness has been pursued through deregulation rather than investment in advanced technological skill. This strategy produces structural conditions within the labour market which make it more difficult to develop a national workforce capable of sustaining the high-skill, high commitment, competitive strategy espoused elsewhere.

The risks of social polarisation

Access to many of the rights of citizenship is gained through economic independence. Education is a right of social citizenship, but its extension is now one of the factors creating ambiguous status for young people. The various forms of intermediate status now experienced by young people are themselves associated with reduced social citizenship rights. They are not linked to adult rights, norms or responsibilities (Jones and Wallace, 1992) and there is increased economic dependence on families as unemployment benefits have been withdrawn. This marks a significant shift in the position of the British young people. Their extended student or trainee status has become closer to European countries such as Germany where there are no expectations of rapid transition to full adult status. But Britain lacks the strong institutional support which has evolved in those countries to secure the position of young people making the transition to adulthood. Added to this historical position, more recent labour market deregulation and the concomitant market oriented policies have had far-reaching implications, producing social polarisation in the ways in which young adults experience transitions into adulthood. The findings reported in this chapter give some indications of policy as experienced. There is a need to look more deeply at opportunity structures and how these are subjectively experienced by young people in transition.

The importance of opportunity structures is reflected in the prevalence of metaphors which attempt to describe the interactions between individuals and structures. The shift of metaphor from 'filling society's niches' to 'navigating perilous waters' provides the context for further discussion of changing opportunity structures and the subjective experiences of individuals.

4 Opportunity structures and status passages: metaphors for transitions to adult life

Metaphors for processes of transition to adult roles, particularly into work, have evolved in ways which reflect both the opportunity structures and the dominant theoretical perspectives of the time. The dominant metaphor for the 1960s was that of filling society's *niches*, reflecting functionalist and developmental perspectives of the time. Chapters 1 and 2 illustrated some ways in which 'growth task' models shaped policies and programmes. These were based on 'normative tasks' which, if completed satisfactorily, guaranteed successful integration into adult roles and adult society. With the majority of young people leaving full-time education at 16, there were three main stratified transitions between school and work, reflected in the themes of the previous chapters. Young people either followed extended careers involving participation in Higher Education, short-term careers in which young people left school in order to enter jobs which provided a period of training (such as apprenticeships and in some white collar positions) or else entered 'careerless' occupations, semi and unskilled jobs which provided little or no training (Ashton and Field 1976). As unemployment increased, Britain developed the 'mixed model' of post-16 education and employment opportunities and occupational allocation through these stratified routes became much less efficient. This was accompanied by emergence of *bridges, routes* and *pathways to work* as dominant metaphors, representing an extension of functionalist perspectives. In the 1980s the metaphor of *trajectory* assumed greater prominence, reflecting structuralist influences. The use of 'trajectory' implies that destinations in the labour market are principally determined by social forces and that labour market destinations are largely outside the control of individual social actors. Drawing the mathematical parallel, in which angle of projection and velocity determine the flight path and the point of landing, social class and cultural capital may be equated with angle and velocity. These are 'trajectories in social space', as Bourdieu (1990) describes them. With the virtual collapse of the youth labour market, transitional outcomes came to be explained more in terms of structural factors such as social class, race and gender, educational attainment and labour market conditions rather than by reference to individual characteristics or aspirations.

Reflecting the reflexive and post-structuralist perspectives of the 1990s metaphors of *navigation* began to emerge strongly; individuals are navigating perilous waters and negotiating their way in a sea of 'manufactured uncertainty'. Success, in this perspective, depends on individual skill and capability, external risks and ability to judge them, or 'living with a calculative attitude to the open possibilities of action' (Giddens 1991, p.28).

All of these metaphors represent ways of analysing and understanding young people's interactions with their social milieu, and the sequence of events between adolescence and adulthood. In order to get a better understanding of the ways in which young people's lives are shaped, it is necessary to explore some of the ways in which opportunity structures contribute to experiences. Moreover, if we accept that individuals assess risk and negotiate opportunities on a subjective level (the navigation model), then it is important to look at some of the ways in which subjective processes affect labour market outcomes. In the first section of this chapter developmental perspectives are examined, with particular reference to learning and schooling, in the second the salient components of opportunity structures are examined. In the final section, the relevance of subjective orientations for an understanding of transitional experiences is assessed.

Filling niches

Educational systems are among the principal social institutions shaping experiences and outcomes. Hill and Monks (1977) described the components of the system as 'youth groups' observing that:

> For society, the function of youth groups is to provide continuity from generation to generation by training young persons in universalistic values.
> For the individual, the function of youth groups is to provide socialisation for adult roles which cannot be learned in the family unit. Three kinds of youth group are to be found in modern societies: schools, youth organisations, and spontaneous groups (p.53).

Developmental theories which predominated in the 50s and 60s have exerted powerful influences in all areas of educational policy and practice, and in all institutions that have a formal role in youth transition. These theories have sought to identify aspects and stages of 'normal' development and common processes in development. Through these, age-appropriate behaviours have come to play a large part in schooling, and the structures of schooling rest on many assumptions about developmental stages and the ways in which young people need to be prepared for successful entry to adult life. They included cognitive, moral, social and physical development. While focusing particularly on the adolescent years, they have become extended and elaborated to post-adolescence as transitions have become elongated. These perspectives have increasingly been challenged on the basis that their assumptions of homogeneity in the age group fail to address differentials of resources and socio-cultural diversity. Their pervasive influence is reflected in the sections which follow.

Interactions with the social milieu

Development of the young person's interactions with the social milieu is seen as fundamental to maturing personal characteristics in developmental perspectives. One characteristic of this interaction has been seen as outstanding: the need of the young person to be liked and valued by peers. Young people strive towards the goal of acceptance in the context of groups whose members they admire and in which they feel that they can best achieve realisation. They gain, in the process, social and personal interdependence between themselves and their chosen associates. The principal functions of the peer group in relation to development in youth have been identified as those of providing a replacement of the family; a stabilising influence; a source of self-esteem; a source of behavioural standards; security; opportunities for practice by doing; opportunities for modelling. The young person, J S Coleman argued in his seminal work on the 'Adolescent Society' (1961, p.3):

> is cut off from the rest of society, forced inward upon his (sic) own age group, made to carry out his whole social life with others his own age, and with his fellows he comes to constitute a small society, one that has most of its important interactions within itself and maintains only a few threads of connection with the outside adult society.

In addition to the need for association and identification with a group, needs emerge for formation of close relations with a few significant friends. In early adolescence, friendships tend to centre on activities, giving way to predominance of personality characteristics as a basis for selection of friends in later stages. The impact of the peer group peaks in mid-adolescence, with susceptibility to peer group influence decreasing with age (Banks et al 1992).

In relationships with adults, family ties are broken to an extent during a 'second individuation' process. Progress in the relationship between the young person and the family of origin is characterised by the young person's increasing and often ambivalent movement towards autonomy. It is frequently a time of friction between parents and adolescents, longer for males than females, but the suggestion that this represents any deep alienation of young adults from parental values and norms is not borne out by research such as that of Friedenberg (1959). In these perspectives young adulthood may be considered a time of striving for status in which the young person is trying to effect a compromise between two desired goals - that of individuality on the one hand, and that of social conformity and acceptance on the other. There is a need for adult recognition.

> Defiance of all adult authority or intolerance of adult-approved standards is often an expression of a struggle to achieve status among his (sic) elders.
>
> (Crow and Crow, 1965, p.170)

The role of the peer group as an agency of learning and stimulus to personal growth among adolescents is well recognised and its potential roles in enabling the young person to develop social confidence and 'leadership ability' underpin many areas of practice in schools, colleges and youth and community organisations.

Developmental processes and 'growth tasks'

The interactional nature of human development was summed up by Cockram and Beloff (1978) thus:

> The process of individual psychological development, interacting with the social context, provides the particular potentiality for change and progress towards mature personality and individual patterns of competence. (p.38)

Change and progress towards mature personality and individual patterns of competence are essentially learning processes. Havighurst (1953), Wall (1968, 1975) and Ausubel (1954), among others, attempted to describe the developmental tasks associated with the learning processes already described, which the young person must achieve in order to become 'successfully integrated' into adult society. Wall's model updated in 1968, presented five 'growth tasks': those of satisfactory construction of a social self, a sexual self, a philosophic self, a vocational self and a physical self. A model presented by Ausubel was based on a similar set of tasks, while Erickson's (1968) developmental theory of adolescence, asserted that all development processes may be considered to be embodied in one central task of adolescence, the construction of an adequate self-identity.

Hamachek argued, in line with Erickson's thesis, that the developmental tasks of adolescence are

> ..... Highly personalised experiences, each of which helps the adolescent define himself (sic) as a person, and develop a recognisable and reasonably predictable self. (1976, p.149)

The ideal self is compared with the social reality of what the person is and what she or he can reasonably expect to be and to do. It is through this process that the self expands and matures (Hurrelmann 1989). In all of these models, the learning processes of adolescence are seen as directed, by the social institutions and structures within which the young person develops, towards achievement of the necessary growth tasks. Failure of the young person to identify with, or achieve, the accepted growth tasks, it is argued, results in withdrawal and alienation, leading to further failure. Success, on the other hand, brings positive benefit, approval and further support for the young person, and leads to continued success and achievement.

> A developmental task ...... is an event that occurs at a certain point in the life of an individual and, with successful achievement, spurs him (sic) to further growth and probably success with later tasks; conversely, failure inhibits growth and leads to disapproval by society and difficulty with later tasks. (Hamachek 1976, p.149)

Growth tasks are, by their nature, necessarily culture-specific and may be considered both to allow the individual to construct a firm self-identity, and hence to achieve the basis for self-fulfilment, and to allow society to fill its 'niches'.

The transition from school to work: learning processes and growth task achievement in the transitional years

The transition to work for the young person leaving the school system at the minimum age may, in developmental perspectives, be construed as transition, while major learning processes are continuing, from a context whose explicit and primary aim is to support and direct the achievement of growth tasks in the young individual, to a context within which such aims are of secondary or minimal importance. This produced concerns of premature 'closure' reflected in reports such as the Crowther report (1959) and in policy debates throughout the 60s and 70s.

The effects of continuing educational participation after 16, and the potential influence of the teacher and professional worker in effecting substantial change and development after completion of basic schooling, became a focus of attention. Interventions 'after sixteen' could be viewed in a number of ways. Borow (1966), for example, pointed out the conditioning effects of the organisation of human resources by the 'controlling adult society' on learning processes in adolescence, and, in particular, on the length of psychological adolescence and the values cultivated during this life stage. Hoffman (1974) argued that parental pressures may also determine choice of career. Choice of high status occupations is clearly associated with high socio-economic status of the family. Among women approval of, and identification with, different types of employment opportunity is influenced, to a large degree, by the home. Values such as work commitment, reflecting the Protestant work ethic, mediate the effects of experience on personal action and are cultivated both through the home and the wider controlling adult society (Furnham 1984: p.198). Some major learning experiences involved in the transition to work, include (a) those produced by 'reality shock' arising from disparities between education and anticipatory socialisation and the reality of day-to-day demands in an occupation, and (b) those arising from crystallisation of hitherto formless interests, aptitudes and aspirations.

In developmental and functionalist perspectives two theses may be developed concerning the interaction between learning and transition to adult roles. Firstly, there is the view that the culture and activities of the school may inhibit learning by undermining self esteem or by producing disengagement. Significant learning is characterised by active involvement and motivation of the learners, and a perception of the worthwhileness of activities undertaken. Leaving school, particularly for those antipathetic towards the culture and activities of the formal system, may be seen as a release from the constraints upon effective learning of the school, presenting potentially new and alternative opportunities for learning and experience.

McCandless and Coop (1979) observe:

> Incidental or experiential learning in the home and workplace results from action and the experiencing of its consequences, and from accepting a role of responsibility for one's actions. The school is an inadequate institution for this sort of learning; in school the cognitive process, mental activity is first. Direct involvement is the last step. (p.368)

It is further argued by Coleman (1974) that the effect of *not* engaging in some form of role offering 'direct involvement' is damaging:

> The consequence of the lengthening of the student role and the active poverty it implies for the young has been an increased restlessness among adolescents. They are shielded from responsibility and they thus become irresponsible. They are held in a dependent status and they do not learn independence. They are kept away from productive work and they are unproductive. (p.10)

McCandless claimed that after 12, schooling can be reduced in importance so that young people have time to learn non-cognitive skills by experience and practice. The 'theory' of adolescent work experience set out by Harris (1977) also embodied this view, stressing the significance, for the various facets of adolescent learning, of experiences of responsibility, of independence, of demonstrated evidence of worth provided by paid work, and of occupational identity. In Germany, Kerschensteiner saw education for citizenship as best postponed until young people had sufficient maturity to 'grasp' its significance. Simons (1996), drawing parallels between Rousseau and Kerschensteiner, observed that

> In the same way that Rousseau would postpone preoccupation with certain subjects, such as history or religion, until the pupil had reached an age when he (sic) had enjoyed a certain amount of experience of life itself, so Kerschensteiner felt that education for citizenship would be more effectively carried out among the older, continuation school pupils, who were already starting on the path to citizenship by the mere fact that they had taken up employment and were thus helping to provide their keep .... At the same time, the instruction in civics would be grasped more readily by these maturer pupils who were beginning to be aware of the role which they and their work played in society. (p.36)

In other words, some forms of learning were dependent upon role transitions having taken place.

The second thesis emphasises extending full-time schooling, as the optimum mode for learning beyond 16; in this perspective transition from school to work at this age and stage of development has been seen as damaging and undesirable. Historically, Miller (1969) argued that the principal effect is to bring to a premature close the 'identification' stage of development and to hasten the 'coping' stage. Young people leaving education early,

> Have an exceedingly short period of mid-adolescence; the speeding-up of identification processes brings many problems and produces little satisfaction for the individual or for society. (p.30)

Herford (1969) observed that young people

> Leave school at a vulnerable stage of metamorphosis. There is a vital need for an adequate supportive, stimulating service for youth, better preparation at school and better continuity of tutorial supervision. (p.156)

Kohlberg and Gilligan (1971) and Piaget (1972), whose theories were highly influential at the time, agreed that the effects of 'early leaving' were damaging since they curtail the opportunities for systematic learning and the cognitive and moral development processes which are so vital to other aspects of development. At a time at which leaving school at 15 or 16 was the 'normal adolescent experience' these were worrying concerns.

The view of proponents of this second thesis was summed up by Hamechek (1976), as follows:

> Just as some individuals remain psychological adolescents most of their lives, others, unfortunately enough, scramble headlong into adulthood without completely working through the tasks of adolescence. An example of this could be the boy who drops out of school before he's either emotionally or educationally ready for economic independence. (p.148)

(The male emphasis again being typical of the time)

In the 1990s, Evans and Heinz (1994) returned to this issue in pointing to the danger of foreclosure of options caused by accelerated transitions of the British system, and the benefits of a extended period of 'soundly-based vocational and general education' for identity development and the maturing personality.

Although the processes and mechanisms operating in the transition from school to work have been focal points of investigation for both sociologists and social psychologists, by the 1970s little evidence had emerged concerning the interaction between learning processes and the achievement of growth tasks on the one hand, and the wider processes of transition on the other. Until the ESRC 16-19 initiative, psychological research in this area had concerned itself primarily with occupational choice and motivation. Psychologists are broadly agreed that earlier life and learning experiences influence occupational decision. It is the nature of that influence which is at issue, and the subsequent effect of occupational choice on continued learning and personal development.

Occupational choice, Ginzberg (1972) argued, is a decision-making process which extends into early adulthood and which cannot be divorced from conditions of employment, and educational needs associated with them. Marcus (1969) stated:

> During a work career, changes in social position affect personal identity, and behavioural stability in turn influences work patterns and institutional reactions ...... adolescents are particularly vulnerable to instability in their set of occupational goals if momentous decisions are reached during periods of rapid transition in their development. (p.169)

In this perspective, new motivation emerges to achieve a certain status in the 'real' world. Individual orientations developed are related to a particular physical and social environment, and a specific set of abilities. The individual seeks the occupation which will satisfy his or her personal orientation.

A range of educational and social variables associated with vocational development has been progressively identified. Self knowledge and knowledge of various occupations affect vocational orientation and there is evidence that occupational choices are consistent with personality types.

The transition process as experienced before the reduction of employment opportunities and the youth unemployment crises of the 1970s and 80s was seen as relatively unproblematic, and almost systematic, as Chester's (1968) model illustrates:

a) Those socialising experiences of the young person which are relevant to education and work, together with
b) Personal variables and
c) Facilities and provision which assist rational choice, lead to
d) The formation of attitudes, expectations and assumptions regarding educational and occupational future.

a), b), c) and d) together provide the explanation for

e) Entry into either (i) a job or (ii) further education, and from this
f) Actual experience leads to a situation of
g) Adjustment/non-adjustment for the young person, leading to a reformulation of d) above, or mobility to another educational or work locus.

Young people who grow up in adverse circumstances have fewer effective options for shaping their lives and careers, while the wider effects of the socio-economic system which structures opportunity and scope for choice was recognised by McCandless (1979), who stated that

> The changing vocational possibilities and inequalities of the social/economic system, as well as the personal or social factors of individual self-concept and status-conferring potential of any job must be included as significant variables in any theory of vocational choice (p.368).

Opportunity Structures[1]

Before moving on to consider the ways in which opportunity structures contribute to transitional experiences, it is necessary to say something about the concept of opportunity structure. In a traditional sense, young people's locations in social structures can themselves be seen as structuring

---

[1] This section has benefited from insights and perspectives provided by Dr Andy Furlong, of Glasgow University, in a joint paper prepared for 'British Youth Research : A New Agenda' Conference, Glasgow 1996.

opportunity. Young people's ascribed characteristics such as class, gender, race, provide them with a set of advantages or disadvantages which affect their transitional outcomes, as do their achieved characteristics such as their school attainments. These can be described as individual attributes.

Area characteristics also have an important effect on transitional experiences and outcomes. The area attribute most commonly referred to in work on youth transitions is that of the labour market. Researchers often concentrate on unemployment rates as indicators of the health of a local labour market (Raffe and Willms 1989 and Gray et al 1992). Researchers have also focused on other attributes such as neighbourhood deprivation (Garner and Raudenbush, 1991) or rurality (Sewell and Haller, 1967), but few researchers have tried to differentiate between the components of area.

In Britain, detailed analyses of areas and labour market effects on transition have been under-developed, as researchers have tended to concentrate on the effects of ascribed attributes such as social class and gender.

Furlong (1996) has pointed out how, given the experience of American sociologists, the lack of emphasis on contextual effects may be justified. In the 1950s and 1960s, Sewell and Hauser spent considerable time examining the ways in which local contexts affected various outcomes but concluded that contextual effects tended to be weak. These conclusions were supported by subsequent American researchers such as Coleman (1961) in his national study of equality of opportunity. Until quite recently, British researchers were arriving at similar conclusions. Garner and colleagues (1987, 1991) attempted to find whether there were significant local variations in the employment prospects of school-leavers in different cities. Using a multi-level model they concluded that while there were neighbourhoods with very high levels of unemployment, it was young people's 'characteristics' which were important, rather than the areas in which they lived. Pockets of relatively high youth unemployment within cities are the product of the low qualifications, disadvantaged family background and other characteristics of the young people who lived there, and of the city-wide labour-market process which disadvantaged young people with these characteristics (p.114). The research showed that in schools, children from the most deprived home neighbourhoods performed less well than children with similar family backgrounds living in more advantaged home neighbourhoods.

More recently, debates have centred on the 'discouraged worker' effect and the extent to which 'staying on' in education is affected by young people's perception of the state of their local labour market. While Raffe and Willms initially found this effect in Scotland, with greater staying on among young people with 'mid-range' qualifications, Gray et al (1992) replicating the analysis in England, did not find a discouraged worker effect, with higher staying on in areas of low unemployment. Further work by Raffe has shown a general weakening of the effects of local labour market conditions on 'staying on'. Evans (1989) has argued that the expectation of staying on in education has become the norm for the average attainer rather than the minority option, reducing the extent to which the labour market is actively considered by those approaching the minimum school leaving age.

These English analyses led Paterson and Raffe (1995) to re-consider the earlier conclusions using data from a range of survey sweeps. In this new analysis, they concluded that the 'discouraged worker' effect of local unemployment rates appeared to decline over the period. This change is explained in terms of a general weakening of the pull from the labour market on young people as job opportunities continued to decline for all young people.

Yet Furlong and Biggart (1995) have suggested that local labour market analysis needs to be developed to move beyond the measurement of unemployment rates. Alternative contextual variables need to be introduced in order to explore the ways in which local conditions of life affect educational participation rates. They have tried to uncover the effects of neighbourhood deprivation on patterns of educational participation and have examined the extent to which young people living in particular areas are handicapped by aspects of their spatial location over and above the levels of disadvantage which may be predicted purely on the basis of individual characteristics.

To summarise Furlong and Biggart's findings, in a model which controls for individual attainment and social characteristics, high unemployment within the local labour market seems to be associated with increased rates of educational participation, confirming the initial findings of Raffe and Willms. On the other hand, it appears as if neighbourhood deprivation is pulling in the other direction and making it more likely that a young person will leave education at the earliest opportunity.

Furlong and Biggart concluded that labour markets and neighbourhoods exert counter-balancing effects. By failing to appreciate the complexity of the relationship, previous researchers have under-estimated the impact of contextual effects on educational participation after sixteen. Unemployment may provide young people with a powerful incentive to remain at school, but neighbourhood deprivation can provide a set of norms and practices which encourage young people to leave school at an early stage. The context within which young people make decisions about future educational participation consists of more than a labour market situation: it also involves a set of communal relationships within which young people develop assumptive worlds and contemplate future events. The effect of high levels of unemployment on educational participation is dependent on the broader context within which it is experienced and perhaps the longterm history of deprivation within a neighbourhood (Furlong and Biggart 1995).

The differences identified by researchers such as Furlong and Biggart highlight the shortcomings of developmental perspectives on transition which 'put forward commonalities based on age, mask social divisions and invite assumptions that young adults approach transitions in the same way, with the same resources, goals and needs' (Wyn 1995). These 'essentialise' youth, minimising differences between groups differently located in social terms. The structures and practices of schooling continue to rest on many of these assumptions about developmental stages and the growth tasks that young people must achieve by certain stages. This implies particular interpretations of the relationship of young people with the wider society. Much of this depends on subjective interpretations of the 'realities' of the labour market and niches available.

Subjectivity in successful transitions from school to work

The relationship between opportunity structures and individual subjectivity can be further explored by focusing on the effects of labour markets on occupational aspirations of young people. This is an area which has been somewhat unfashionable in British sociology over the last couple of decades. As the British youth labour market collapsed, sociologists began to challenge the extent to which individual aspirations had any impact on occupational outcomes. Roberts (1985) in particular argued that occupational aspirations were often little more than subjective interpretations of objective labour market realities. For many young people there are few meaningful choices and the sorts of jobs they enter depend on local opportunities.

It is important to say from the outset that calling for a more detailed analysis of individual subjectivity is not trying to make out that individuals have control over transitional processes. Rather it accepts the point made by Giddens (1991) that factors which influence individual outcomes tend to operate via the subjectivity of the agents concerned and argues that through a better understanding of the subjective dimensions of social reproduction we can learn more about structures of opportunity and individual agency.

This chapter has shown that there has been a fairly long tradition of studying the ways in which people develop aspirations within the constraints of the family and the educational system. Developmental approaches have highlighted the ways in which individuals achieve a vocational maturity through their experiences in childhood and adolescence and explain ways in which aspirations become more realistic over time and are brought into line with expectations.

A number of writers have emphasised the ways in which, during their early teens, boys and girls move through a stage of active exploration in which they try to 'locate' themselves within the constraints of the society in which they are growing up. As their ideas about their academic potential develop, their occupational aspirations become more refined: certain sections of the labour market come to be seen as outside their reach or requiring too much effort to attain, while other jobs come to be seen as lacking in prestige and falling below a level which they find acceptable.
Young people also develop ideas about the appropriateness of certain occupations for a person of their sex and this further limits their aspirations (Gottfredson, 1981). Thus occupational aspirations tend to occupy what Gottfredson terms a 'zone of acceptable alternatives' and this subjective interpretation of the relationship between opportunities and ability affects their planned routes through education and into the labour market.
Furlong and Biggart have shown that although young people have a basic awareness of the level and type of opportunities available in their local labour market, the industrial structure of labour markets has a relatively small effect on aspirations once other sources of variation have been accounted for. For males, neighbourhood deprivation and rurality have an important depressing effect on aspirations, although these effects are much weaker for females.

Social reproduction and youth cultures

Intergenerational transmission of values and the work roles between parents and their children was highlighted in studies which examined emergent youth cultures in the 70s. The interplay of generation and social class, newly emphasised by Hall and Jefferson (1976), was crucial in these perspectives, emphasising the way in which power structures reinforce and reproduce social inequalities from generation to generation. They also emphasise the 'reaction of alienation' in which young people actively turn away, or engage in opposition, alienated from school culture which is at odds with the values of their family of origin and community. Anti-school cultures reinforce their social position and ensure that they are trapped into working class jobs which perpetuate their powerlessness (Willis, 1977, Mac-an-Ghaill (1996) argues that working-class males are the new disadvantaged. With none of the traditional markers of adulthood of access to real work available to them, they have been systematically subjected to new forms of social control by 'new right' policies which redefined the workplace in terms of competences and made the 'qualifications' the central means of control of trainees.

Women tended to be invisible in the early analyses, which focused on working class male youth, and often failed to address and explain the diversity of experience of social groups differently located in the power structures of society. Variables of race, gender and disability which are fundamentally linked with power structures and interact with social class in complex ways, have been introduced into theories of social and cultural reproduction and have changed them. For example, Griffin (1985) studied the female counterpart of male youth cultures, while writers such as Walby (1986) examined other aspects of the social structure of inequality, with reference to concepts such as patriarchy.

Successful transitions from school to work involve a complex interplay between labour market structures and individual subjectivity. At one level we can use longitudinal studies of youth to 'map' the correlates of successful transitions and processes of exclusion by looking at the likely outcomes of following different routes between school and work.

However, subjective processes have an important bearing on labour market outcomes. Contradictions were found by Bates and Riseborough (1993) in their ethnographic studies of young people following college-based vocational courses, between the extent of manifest influence of class and family background on the young people studied and their own 'notable degree of reflexivity, a capacity for creative reconstruction of biography in terms of personal progress and fulfilment' (p.6). While young people experienced choice and control in their immediate contexts, Bates and Riseborough concluded that their attitudes and opinions may be 'over-individualistic' as a result of their limited experience and ability to make the kinds of comparisons between groups which lead sociologists to other conclusions. Belief in individual choice was important for maintenance of sense of purpose, and 'fate', Bates argues, tends to be reconstructed as choice, facilitated by the values of personal reflexivity and self-actualisation. Nevertheless there was evidence that young people were loosening social ties and connections and making themselves 'the centre of their own life plans, and the patterns of experience were not readily explained by either structural or social reproduction theories. Explanations in terms of educational experience and media influence had not 'settled the score' between human agency and social structure (Bates 1993, p. 29-30, 82). New theoretical advances are dependent on our ability to integrate a greater understanding of the subjective determinants of 'success' with a better knowledge of the salient components of opportunity structures.

Coles (1996) argues that there are three interconnected transitions to be considered in the housing, family and school-work domains.

> ..... Each of the three main youth transitions involve the interplay of two sides of a 'careers equation'. These two sets involve decision making by both young people and their families or surrogate families and those charged with responsibility for the social and economic context in which they grew up. It is important to understand both sides of this equation. Only by focusing attention on both can one begin to appreciate either the micro-patterns of individual career development or the macro-patterns of 'youth' as a general and socio-structural phase within the life-course (p. 71).

In the theoretical perspectives of social and cultural reproduction 'normative growth tasks' and 'career' trajectories themselves reflect the operation of power structures, serving to include, recognise and reinforce the achievements of those favourably positioned while excluding and reinforcing the disadvantages of others. Society structures opportunity, shapes experiences and outcomes and sets parameters for participation. Findings of the 16-19 Initiative, in the late 80s, provided further evidence in support of this, in its findings on 'career trajectories' (Banks et al 1992). In the 1990s, transitions became much less predictable, more fragmented. Has this resulted in a greater number of predetermined trajectories, or has transition become more subject to the individual's ability to negotiate changing structures of opportunity?

Individualisation

Analyses of the contemporary situation of young adults is showing increasing fragmentation of opportunities and experience; the processes of youth are highly differentiated, reflecting and constructing social divisions in society in much more complex ways. Neither developmental/functionalist theories nor structuralist theories are adequate to explain these phenomena.

As these diversified and differentiated patterns have emerged, so have new theoretical perspectives centred on the 'life course', individualisation, and 'focal' theories. These have gained ground, as theories with enhanced power to explain the phenomena of early adult life and work transitions (Figure 4.1).

The 'life course' used to be organised around employment history. It is now becoming much more complex and differentiated, less subject to the power of the work ethic, and it has been argued that life courses will soon be seen in terms of educational or self-actualisation biographies rather than 'careers'. Trajectories in social space as described by Bourdieu (1990) are 'losing their clarity of form' according to Alheit (1995). Class, gender,

METAPHORS: FILLING NICHES (short transitions) PATHWAYS (extended transitions) THEORETICAL CONSTRUCTIONS: Role change; stage therories EMPHASIS: Normative tasks (age-related)giving stability, identity and certainty if tasks completed successfully	METAPHORS: TRAJECTORIES THEORETICAL CONSTRUCTIONS: Reactions of alienation Social and cultural reproduction of roles EMPHASIS: Social structures and power relations

METAPHOR: NAVIGATIONS

THEORETICAL CONSTRUCTIONS:
Focal theory; life course theory; biographical construction, individualisation.

EMPHASIS:
Negotiation of structures of opportunity and risk, giving sources of stability or instability in the life course

Figure 4.1: Theoretical perspectives on transitions

ethnicity become important as 'differential resources' in the life course, not as determinants of outcomes, with collective biographical patterns obscured by individual risk situations. The fact that people feel that they act autonomously and independently over their own biographies is not necessarily at odds with the view that much of the biography continues to be structured by external factors. While individuals' beliefs that they have some control over their fate is one of the driving forces within society Roberts (1995) argues that the 'consequences of choices were trivial' compared with the extent to which prospects were dependent on social class, school attainments, gender and jobs available in local labour markets.

The issue now is the interplay between structure and agency arising from 'manufactured uncertainty' - uncertainty created by acceleration of the information and knowledge-based society and the increase and diversity of 'risk' situations felt in individual lives. What evidence is there of growing 'individualisation' arising from this interplay of structure and agency?

Some evidence has emerged that young people have become more critical of bad jobs; they want to do work which is personally satisfying. This is particularly marked in the case of young women who are incorporating employment in their life plans in unprecedented ways. Evidence from western Germany (Baethge 1989) showed young people using the extended and supported period of transition to develop work orientations which look for interest and challenge above income, job security and promotion. Comparisons of the actual experiences of young people over time have enabled some testing of the social theory of individualisation in a comparative context (Evans and Heinz 1994).

This study found evidence for the following transition behaviours:

- *Strategic:* This is planned, very often linked to a clear-cut vocational choice and to definite occupational goals, and most often found among young people who were moving towards higher education, and some in training for skilled occupations.
- *Step-by-step:* Occupational choice is not very clear cut, there is a process of searching for an interesting occupation. The one taken up usually is not tied to a definite occupational goal. This transition behaviour is found mainly among young people who are in trajectory II (skilled) and I (academic).
- *Taking chances:* This consists of occupation-related activities that are characterised by testing and following interests, either by confronting oneself with demanding training or educational processes, or by following a specific aptitude. This transition behaviour was found among young people from all four trajectories, but mainly young people from trajectory III (transitional programmes) were taking chances.
- *Wait and see*: This is characterised by an attitude of 'learned helplessness', that is one is happy if the situation does not get worse; there is the dim hope that there will be a lucky moment in the future. It is mainly young people from trajectory IV (unemployed/under-employed) and some from trajectory III (transitional programmes) who look back to a transition history that is marked by disappointments and failures.

The extent to which young people have succeeded in developing longer-term occupational goals depends not only on their past socialisation in family and school but also to a large degree on the way their identity formation was linked to challenges and rewarding experience in the passage to employment itself. It makes a big difference whether a young person embarks on the risky voyage in a clearly defined progression of experience and qualifications, based on his or her decisions, or in a diffuse, short-term arrangement which is reactive to immediate job demands. Self-confidence seems to arise out of success in completion of tasks, from vocational choice to labour market entry, and in coming to terms with changing work structures in personal decision-making. The 'strategic' and the 'taking chances' approach to transition are expressions of this kind of active individualisation. There is a more passive kind of individualisation in which the young person is carried along in socially accepted transition patterns, without a sense of ultimate goal. Lack of resources acts against risk-taking which could result in career 'damage'. Transition behaviour which is characterised by a 'step-by-step' or a 'wait-and-see' pattern is linked to a passive kind of individualisation.

The optimum mode of transition can be described as 'active individualisation', that is autonomy in the choice of goals and in ways to achieve them. This contrasts with the passive forms of individualisation, in which goals are weakly defined and strategies to achieve them uncertain. Far from controlling their own transition, young people find themselves propelled on to a downward occupational spiral into unskilled work and unemployment. In both countries these modes of individualisation and the career patterns that characterise them have structural foundations in gender, race and social class. Those on the 'top' trajectories, typically high achievers with strong social support, tend to the active mode; those on the bottom trajectories, typically low achievers with weak social networks, tend more to passivity. There is some evidence that the English system encourages active risk-taking rather than strategic approaches, by surrounding young people, unevenly, with job opportunities. The German system can actively promote strategic approaches by surrounding young people with a reasonably transparent framework of institutional support, but only if the learning and support processes encourage active behaviours within this framework. Female modes of transition also tend more to passivity than male modes and, because of the perceived conflicting demands of a domestic career, operate through a much narrower range of occupational choices.

If individualisation is an inverse measure of the extent to which individuals, in adult life, still know, live and work alongside those from the community in which they grew up or have life patterns and experiences in common with them, then individualisation has been a trend for most of the twentieth century in many geographical regions (Roberts 1995).

Alternatively, if individualisation is conceptualised as the process whereby individuals perceived the need to map out their own routes through a confusing array of opportunities and take increasing responsibility for the risk of failure in this process, then there is evidence (Rudd 1997) that young people *are* experiencing such a process in unprecedented ways.

Young people's experiences are shaped by the interplay of socialising and structural influences and the elements of subjectivity, choice and agency:

> A belief in personal control is a central part of the self-identity of young people. Young people in the 1990s have a very strong belief in personal choice: they can do more than push boundaries around, they really believe that they are shaping their own destinies ..... generally young people seem to have

a greater belief in choice than they had ten or twenty years ago (Rudd 1997, p.238).

Agency is to do with cultivating the *belief* that choices are possible and implies active individualisation and possession of the associated action competences. Support services in the school and beyond can play a role in encouraging active or passive modes of individualisation and the kind of career and life patterns that flow from them, as well as in influencing the extent of personal agency. The personal, social and institutional support services that young people use in making their transition choices interact. For any policy to be effective, it needs to be holistic, taking account of not only the young people themselves but also the whole of the social and educational framework in which they are embedded.

5 Winners and losers in transition

The previous chapter discussed, from a number of theoretical perspectives, that ways in which career and life patterns develop through the interplay of individual needs, motives, capabilities and the social structures for transition. State control of economic status in early adult life has increased throughout the latter part of the 20th Century, as transitions towards independence have become elongated within a framework of education and training provision and labour market options. Educational institutions play a major part in shaping the course of lives, but so also do structures for social support and the labour market, and the transition behaviours which young adults employ in negotiating these structures. Access to many citizenship rights is through economic independence with citizens' rights and obligations increasingly identified with, and tied to, employment status.

Together labour markets, social support systems and institutions interact to produce the structures of 'opportunity' and 'risk' experienced by individuals and social groups. Constantly shifting, these are increasingly provisional and reversible in their effects. What makes for successful and unsuccessful transitions in this context? Who are the winners and losers in the early stages of careers and the adult life course?

Successful transitions

The first example of successful transition comes from the academic trajectory into the labour market. *Stuart* is a case of strategic decision-making and career building. He did not consider job-seeking at either 16 or 18 years of age, but was set to follow the A level route at sixth form college, with a view to University entrance. This was the way of his peer group: 'both for me and for contemporaries we all aimed for University and went that way'. His parents had also actively wanted him to stay in education. Choosing a suitable higher education course was not influenced by particular job aspirations: 'I knew I would be looking for a technical job but that was all'. The course he chose brought together 'Physics with the technical side' and 'to do them combined there was only one place': he chose to do Physics with opteoelectronics at Birmingham University. He sought and gained a local company sponsorship with a bursary plus employment every vacation to work in the R and D laboratories. One value of the scholarship was that 'I never had to look for vacation work, I just wrote to Company R saying when I could start and when I would finish. I worked in the R and D laboratories. I though the exposure to a work environment was particularly valuable'. He found the latter through 'picking up a leaflet at school' and following this up himself by writing to the company. He took a year out from his degree course to work with the same company, finding the money and experience useful. This 'year out' was not an industrial year, on or part of the course - he chose to 'take a year out' before the final year. He felt that his main gains from this were personal development and skills in working with people which would be useful 'wherever work involves interaction with others'. He also considered himself to have had a lot of experience in using Information Technology, gained at home and through school, college and work. Jobseeking began in earnest in his final year at University, with the 'milk round' and speculative applications to all optoelectronics suppliers, most of which resulted in rejections because his approach was 'on the off-chance'. He obtained employment with British Telecom, one of four applications he had made through the 'milk round', and was working on the quality and reliability of optical fibres. He talked of the value of his degree in the way it had prepared him to approach and tackle problems. His general job intentions were to get into management in research and development, and these were maintained as his immediate job intentions within British Telecom. His interests in sports were also framed in terms of his belief that 'sports keep both mind and body fit for top performance'.

He rated opportunity to use initiative, good career prospects and friendly atmosphere at work as the most important in choosing a job. From a middle-class family, he reported himself very satisfied with his family life, relationships and friends, and did not want his job to interfere with his private life. His self-presentation was confident and articulate. He felt his career had so far been successful and was very sanguine about his future prospects. He expected to work for additional qualifications in the future and thought it very likely that he would move to a different part of the country. Quite interested in politics, he would vote and was very dissatisfied with the government. He exhibited a *strategic* approach to life, taking actions in pursuit of progressively focused goals. He had suffered no setbacks at the time of interviews, in contrast with Jane, whose story follows.

Jane provides an example of a mixed employment transition (upward, then stagnant). She achieved a successful build-up of clerical and secretarial skills leading to a supervisory position, despite set-backs, but was then placed in a position which was not using her skills fully.

Jane's aim had always been to 'go out to work' at 16. She did not consider any alternatives which would involve staying in full-time education, although she had achieved reasonable qualifications. She operated within narrow gender stereotypical alternatives, with 'shop' or 'office' as the options: 'I only wanted to work in an office, definitely not a shop ... I just wrote to lots and lots of companies'. She wrote to many companies, seeking office work. She eventually took a job with British Rail, who trained her as a VDU wages input clerk. After a year she suffered a major set-back when she was made redundant on closure of the BR Engineering Works. She went to the Careers Service and again applied for many jobs. She was unemployed for three months, before finding a job with an underwriting and reinsurance firm as a word-processing operator. She was retrained from scratch by the company, through in-house training, and worked her way up to senior operator and deputy supervisor. In the late 1990s the company was taken over. Many were made redundant under the new management. Jane was among those retained by the Company, but she was demoted back into the 'typing pool'. While she kept her higher grading and was well paid for what she was doing, she found the job so boring that she wanted to leave and was looking actively for suitable vacancies through the local paper but finding very little, with many companies in the Swindon area also reducing in size and making workers redundant. She had accumulated not only word-processing but also reception and switchboard skills, and hoped to get more involved with desk-top publishing. She had recently married and intended having a family.

> 'I've only been married six months and we may have a family by then. I would likely go back after having children, I would look for the same type of work ..... for example, I would like to do desk-top publishing, we are pushing for that at work as we just got page makers ..... but I also do reception, so I could do reception and switchboard.'

She was living independently, with her spouse, and had taken on a mortgage. Parents were still her main source of advice to whom she would turn if she needed to talk about worries. Her spare time was most often spent with her partner, but she still spent time with friends and workmates. She had no affiliations to clubs, societies or political parties, although she was 'quite interested' in politics and had voted. She saw 18 as the threshold age for most 'adult' activities such as drinking and going on holiday with friends rather than parents, although she saw 16 as the 'right' age to have a full-time job. She thought that the government did not do enough for young people as regards jobs and housing, and that there should be more training for jobs at reasonable wages, more employers willing to give people a chance! At the same time she felt she paid too much in taxes.

Given a list of political tasks and challenges related to the environment, education, equal opportunities, education and training, she rated all (except uniting Europe) as important to her. Jane was pro-active in job-seeking, and had a broad sense of the direction in which she wanted to go. She had overcome setbacks to some extent by taking action to remedy the situation, although her present endeavours were not producing the outcome she wanted, given the general conditions of the labour market. Her attitude to work was to get the job done while she was there, but keep it firmly in place and it certainly did not occupy a central place in her life interests. 'I'm faithful to the job when I'm there but when I leave, go out the door, I forget it.' She had developed an occupational identity but work was not the central interest or source of fulfilment to her at this stage in her life.

Another example of a transition in which setbacks were overcome is provided by *Carol*. Carol was unemployed for an unusually long period in a relatively buoyant labour market in the late 1980s. She spent a full 12 months unemployed, living with her parents. Her father had been an 'early' school leaver although her mother had extended her education to the age of 17. Carol had stayed on at college 'to save myself looking for a job' and had successfully retaken examinations previously failed at school. She also followed a Certificate in Pre-Vocational Education (CPVE) which she said had 'opened her eyes a lot' and made her reconsider her original aim of working in social care. She now realised the disadvantages, she said, and the experience of College had generally helped her to mature.

> ....That opened my eyes a lot. That did, we did, I mostly did child care and actually going out in the community and actually helping people. Like I did a play group in the mornings and just listening to the mothers talking about what they'd experienced and what their day was like was a total eye-opener to me. Good grief, you'd done all that in one morning, I thought. It was a real eye-opener. And I went to work with old people and that startled me as well. They were left in their houses, mostly sort of what, 6 days a week and they only get a day out, maybe an afternoon to talk to other old people. They must be lonely. It was some eye-opener, it really was.... So yes, that's where my figures came from because they taught me about bank accounts and HP. Because before, you don't think about HP. You think, oh I can pay this off and then you realise how much interest you're paying. I thought that's an

awful lot. It would be quicker to save up and then buy it rather than go to HP so that taught me never to buy anything on HP.

It was more, how can I put it. They treated you more like an adult at college. They were sort of on Christian name terms and they would do anything to help whereas at school or at my school, they tend to be very prim and proper. Things were done sort of, they taught us mostly from the blackboard at school so of course you just copied it down and read the occasional book and that was it. Whereas at college it was much more relaxed.

It was, I don't know if it was growing up as well, I really don't know. I was quite shy at school until I left school and then of course I mixed with different people and if you discuss things in a group, you tend, people tend to listen to you, so of course, you then tend to talk more because they're listening, whereas at school we never had the chance to discuss anything.

She decided she wanted to work in an office, but was unemployed for a year. She reported writing 5 or 6 letters a week, getting no response, which she found 'very depressing'.

I went straight from college on to the dole queue.

Interviewer: How did that affect you do you think during that time?

Carol: .... very depressed by the end. I was writing 5 or 6 letters a week, no it got to 5 or 6 letters a day. I was enclosing stamped/addressed envelopes and you'd never hear from the employer. Never hear. It was a horrible feeling. I'll never forget it. Waiting at the door for the postman to see what you've got. I'd never go through it again. No, it's not a very nice feeling.

Interviewer: No. Do you think you were getting enough direction in what to do during that time?

Carol: No, because I got no direction at all. It was all, if I looked in the newspaper or kept my ears open and the radio and that was about it. I did it all myself and it takes a lot to keep your spirits up, to say yes you will eventually get a job after all this effort. Yes.

Interviewer: Do you think, when you were moving around, do you think that you actually had a direction of where you were going or were you just looking for a better job?

Carol: I was just looking for a better job. A bit more money and something else I could do. And something I could move up into.

She eventually obtained a job, working as an office junior in a solicitor's office, and worked long hours for low pay.

Interviewer: What did you leave for?

Carol: I was doing too much. I started at 8.30 in the morning till about 9 at night.

Interviewer: Right. How much were you paid when you were doing that?

Carol: £3,000 a year I think I was on. It went up, by the time I'd left. I started on some £3,000 a year and by the time I left it went up about four or five hundred I think. £4,500. So it was very low wages.

Interviewer: Did you feel exploited?

Carol: I did, I felt very exhausted by the end of the day and I'd just about had enough, and then one day I just sort of thought I'm going to look for a new job and that was it. That was the first job I went for and I got it.

She then changed jobs twice, eventually becoming a switchboard operator/receptionist at a magistrates court.

I've become a lot more independent. I can do things. I can talk to people on the telephone and I can get the results that I want to hear. I've become more independent, able to work on my own. You're actually trusted to work on your own, I mean, you can work on your own initiative. You can go however fast or however slow you want.

Interviewer: How do you think you've actually gained there, would you say, through your own...

Carol: I've learnt a lot more because I'm always inquisitive, which I wasn't before. I'm willing to ask questions on how does this work and why do I do that and if I press that, what happens. So yes, I've become a lot more, sort of independent in that sort of way.

I didn't have a bank account until I started work. I didn't need one for the solicitor's because we were paid weekly so it came as a shock working with the court, having to be paid monthly. Having a bank account it came as rather a shock, especially with people sort of, oh you can have a credit card, you can do this, you can do that and it suddenly hits you that you don't know anything about it. You're not very prepared sort of moneywise, you're not taught to save or put things by or allow for bills and it comes as an awful shock to have this money going in the bank. You think, yes, I'm rich and suddenly it has to last 4 or 5 weeks. You think how on earth am I going to budget for this. And no, I didn't think it was very good starting off at all.

While her job at the Magistrate's Court offered better salary and prospects, she did not herself perceive the opportunities. She felt that she had got into 'the law' by accident.

Interviewer: What did they (the Careers Service) do at school then?

Carol: A lot was about the Forces. Or it was very, the girls got cookery and so on and the boys tended to get engineering and scaffolding, you know building? If you went in for anything sort of different? 'Cause I remember one of the girls wanted to join the Air Force and it was very frowned upon. She wasn't at all helped. So it's very, very stereotyped. It's like in, I did child care at school and they was all girls. I did cookery at school and they was all girls, and yet when I did woodwork they looked as if to say what on earth is she doing. It was very stereotyped.

Interviewer: Do you think that if you had had access to good Careers Educational Service you would have changed your mind at all, at the time?

Carol: Yes. Yes I do. I definitely don't think I'd end up in law. I don't know what else I would've gone into but I definitely wouldn't have ended up in law.

Interviewer: Would you think about perhaps studying 'A' Level law at some point?

Carol: No, no. To be honest I can't see myself going that far with law. I'm quite happy at the moment just being the admin and helping everybody else out. I don't really want to go as far as court or anything higher, 'cause there are so many varying tasks I've got in the office now, it would be nice to sort of do a few more different tasks that I haven't got to yet.

It was not a conscious career choice, she did not believe that employers value qualifications and she did not see herself doing much more. She currently had a passive construction of occupational identity, with rather fatalistic attitudes but had 'taken chances' in changing jobs when she found herself in an unsatisfactory situation. She was, however, 'very interested' in politics, a member of a Trade Union and felt strongly about social and economic issues which were 'very important to her' although they did not spur her to active participation in politics or related organisations.

So far, our cases have eventually overcome setbacks. Graham, by contrast, had a relatively promising start, but soon experienced difficulties which led to unemployment and unskilled casual work picked up where he could find it.

Graham had completed an ONC in engineering but made no attempt to get vacation work or the kind of placement experience which had led to opportunities for others. He did not obtain a job in engineering but rather took a speculative job offer to work as a trainee veneer preparer. He had literally been 'stopped in the street' by a neighbour who had offered him a job in the wood trade.

> *Interviewer:* What was that connection?
>
> *Graham:* My, it was walking down the street actually. I'd left college and I was walking down the street one day, when a neighbour said have you found a job yet. I said, well, no not yet. She goes, well would you like one. I said, yes alright then. She said I don't know what you'll get but it'll be in the wood trade. I said that's fair enough. So anyway. There were no jobs at the time like there is now and I said yes I'll have one, so I ended up doing veneering.

He was trained for this 'on-the-job', and turned down the possibility of evening classes. He felt a school project had helped him with relevant skills:

> Yes. The veneering I started when I left college
>
> *Graham:* I had no clue about veneering, well I did, I'd done a project for it at school and it was totally appalling, and you know, I didn't know anything about it but afterwards I learnt so much about it. I think, my God, if I could only do that project again, you know. It was a good introduction to the wood trade. The skills I learnt in it was how to look at wood and distinguish the good from the bad, like. Also to look at what you're doing, was a very important factor, I was doing boardroom tables and the guillotine was 2.4, no 3 metres long and we were, sometimes had to turn tables over at 6 metres long, in 2 pieces. So you'd only cut it to fit in the guillotine like to cut the leaves, the veneer, and then you had to look at the pattern, so you'd get a nice pattern.

He moved to another firm for higher pay, still as a veneer preparer.

> I moved firms. I moved from GR to WJ. They were, like, supposed to be the best in Europe ... do some real good work here. I couldn't put my efforts into it. I got there and I found their work was just appalling. It was, their quality was bad and you know. It's no wonder I got ... got laid off in the end. About a third of us got laid off and I ... management was appalling. People weren't even putting the effort into it. I was trying to put the effort and people were just laughing when I was telling them, little things to get the job right and better ... in the first place, you know. I said don't laugh this is how you, you know.
>
> Get decent managers in. Listen to the people on the shop floor. We had a Worker's Council there but they wouldn't listen to the Veneer Shop. I don't know what they were scared of ... they just laughed at us so we just gave in on that one. Well, if I had to go back there I ... I'd hand my notice in on the first day I was back. I wouldn't want to go back there, 'cause they wouldn't listen

to workers. The Managing Director, he can tie you in knots he can. He wouldn't listen to you. He was a good enough bloke, he pays the best money in town like, you know he pays you a Christmas bonus. Just before Christmas we all have pizzas and a couple of crates of beer. If he wants to he can tie you in knots.

He was made redundant, and after a short period of unemployment obtained temporary unskilled warehouse work, through an employment agency, while looking for work as a production operator.

> I got bored with being on the dole. I was on the dole for about a month, month and a half, and I thought this is no good, there wasn't no jobs about so I went into an agency and said you got a job and that was at 11 o'clock and I was just settling down for a bit of kip on the settee and they rang me up and said would you go in at 2 o'clock.

After a large number of applications, he had just been interviewed for a job wiring cable. He believes that this is the 'way in' and that you then have prospects to move on. Longer term he did not see himself 'staying in the same industry for four years at a time'.

He had been looking for other work even before being made redundant. He was generally critical of management attitudes and also of the attitudes of some workers. His approach was that he likes to be busy, and applies himself to the task in hand, both at work and when unemployed. He 'loved working with wood' but now felt he had done that and wanted to move on to something else.

His attitudes to education and training were mixed: he saw his ONC as useful:

> Yes, 'cause it's an engineering-based firm. It might give me an edge over the competitors, you know. But I think education's a load of bollocks anyway until you're about 26.

> Because you don't know the value of it until you've actually been in a trade for a couple of years.

> *Interviewer*: Why do you think, do you think you need the experience of the trade or...

> *Graham:* I think you need the time in the job to look back and say well I wish I'd done, you know. I can learn more, now I know a bit more. I can learn it easier and better. When I went on to the engineering course, you know, after the first weeks I thought well if I'd known this at school I'd have passed my 'O' level Physics with an 'A'.

He saw his college experiences as different:

> Because, I ... how they put it over but it seemed like it was more adult than, you know, it was. You done it because you wanted to. He thought you was more of an adult and so you wanted to try and beat him like.
>
> Try and prove that you could be. You could learn ... School was a load of crap ... taught you to read and write but, I mean, the books were out of date and nothing. They wouldn't have books like this in the library, you know. Anything that people were starting to get into. Like, Poldark series for some people and Leslie Thomas, Tom Sharpe, you know. Which is what people started getting into about our age, like 14 and 15. They just didn't have anything like that in the library. You had, the book reviews you had for your English, oh dear they were terrible.
>
> *Interviewer:* What were they?
>
> *Graham:* There was Mice and Men, such a boring book.
>
> *Interviewer:* Yes. So you think that they were really lagging behind time-wise in a sense.
>
> *Graham:* Yes. Not keeping up to date, mind you since this government's been in we haven't had the money have we.
>
> *Interviewer:* No, no? You mean cut back?
>
> *Graham:* Yes. You learn out of chemistry books which are 20 years old, and physics books you know. We used to see who could get the lowest date, you know, the oldest book and that.

He did not like the town of Swindon, disliked violence and antagonistic behaviour, so stuck to his own area, with his friends. He enjoyed activities such as camping, venture scouting and aircraft modelling. He reported that he was quite interested in politics and would probably vote for the Labour Party.

Graham illustrates a construction of occupational identity which is almost totally reactive. He has no overall sense of direction, although he regarded the opportunity to use initiative and the possibility of becoming better qualified as more important than 'choosing' a job. He did one thing, then another, according to what came up, what was available. He was, however, sure that he wanted to work with his hands, regarding Swindon as being full of 'paper pushers'. He considered himself to be a 'hard worker' and a cheerful person, although he is uneasy about various aspects of social life and his dislike of Swindon is tied up, to some degree, with his apparent lack of clarity about his own identity.

> Once you're with certain friends you know you don't go outside the boundary unless it's with the opposite sex like. It's terrible, you look at a person in Swindon on a Saturday night you've got a thick lip or a broken nose you know. I hate Swindon. There's no friendliness here. They've imported a lot of people over the last 10 years from London and the north. You go first day at work any firm, I dunno what it's like round your area, no one speaks to you do they? You sit down and you know people give you bad looks and you're thinking what I have done now and then you realise you've sat in someone's place you know? The second day I started at c.... you know, I come in I goes good morning chaps and chapesses, they looked at me stupid. I goes what's up did I say something wrong, cheer up. Life's a joke and all this you know. They thought I was mental 'cause I was a happy soul sort of thing. I wanted to make friends and laugh.

The ability to maintain an optimistic and cheerful attitude under adverse circumstances was found among our sample of young people particularly in Liverpool. *Alan*, by contrast, emphasised the depression stemming from his experiences in the labour market.

Alan had been unemployed more or less for the last twelve months. He had worked at a carpet warehouse as part of a YTS scheme and was taken on afterwards. He worked there full time for four years, then the owner retired and the manager took over. Alan did not get along so well with the manager and was employed by him only on a casual basis, while he was claiming social security. Despite his lack of enthusiasm for the job at the warehouse, which he saw as hard, badly paid and without prospects, Alan found unemployment very difficult to cope with. He also mentioned financial problems, the constant need to borrow and pay back money, the restrictions on social life caused by lack of money. He also stressed the depression resulting from unemployment and the lack of structure to one's day:

> Takes about a month like a holiday, just get out of bed at about ten o'clock. Didn't have to worry about work the next day. Then I went through a phase of staying up all night, sitting up all night and going to bed in the morning, about eight o'clock in the morning, and get up about four and stay up straight through again ... nothing to do, bored.

His depression had led him to act violently at home:

> Yeah, does get you down ... one day ... I was going upstairs, just used to stay in me room then, I couldn't open the door ... I just got this mad rush of like anger and just booted the door through, a glass door, I nearly chopped me foot off. That cost me twelve quid to get it fixed so I never done it again. That's the way it gets you though.

Alan systematically deprecated his qualifications. We have already seen his reactions to unemployment. Despite asserting that he had a good relationship with his mother, and mentioning mates and drinking companions, he felt himself to be socially isolated:

> I take my dog out for a walk, that's it. I just take the dog out all day, there's nothing else to do ... it's my only friend at the moment. That's the only thing I'd be sorry for leaving Liverpool for, poor dog would miss me.

As we have seen some young people stressed money, either directly, or in terms of providing for their leisure activities. Some stressed security, such as Alan, who despite his dissatisfaction with the warehouse job had obviously stayed there for reasons of security, a tactic which had been successful:

> No, I just stayed there like. Once I'm in a job I just get on with it. I don't really try and get out of it. I just stick it as long as I can. I mean, the warehouse, it was bad like but I thought oh well a job's a job isn't it.

Others attached importance to the manifestation of change in status as they got older. Alan said:

> Yeah, we just talk like mates, you know, not like a son and a mum like.
>
> *Interviewer:* How did this happen. When did you make that transition?
>
> *Alan:* Just happened when I was about sixteen like ... just after I left school really, I could smoke in the house.

Alan also mentioned that his relationship with his mother had got better since he had become unemployed:

> Since I've come on the dole I seems to have got better like in a way. We have a good laugh all the time. Its 'cause she's stuck with me all the time, she has to put up with me laughs or not.

This more independent relationship vis à vis parents was reflected in the fact that many young people preferred to discuss problems with their siblings and friends rather than their parents.

Historically, geographical location is regarded as less significant for individuals set for Higher Education, who have been regarded as oriented towards national rather than local labour markets although this is changing with the expectation of entry and greater emphasis on attending the institution local to your home. The case of Laura illustrates that this is not necessarily so. *Laura's* interview is interesting for several, sometimes surprising, ways in which place can affect an individual's biography. Laura had just finished a degree in Business Studies and Spanish and had been looking round for a job, so far without success. She had just been looking in the local labour market however because she was engaged to a Liverpool

taxi-driver who had never lived outside the city and was reluctant to leave it. Laura was aware that given the nature of her qualifications her career opportunities would be better if she left home but she was in something of a dilemma because of her fiancé's attachment to the city. Clearly there was a potential conflict here, with the possibilities of the fiancé yielding to Laura's wishes, of the pair splitting up, or of Laura remaining and looking for work in the local labour market. Laura was one of several young people, both English and German, who mentioned that their relationships with their parents had improved when they had moved away from home.
In her case a move away from home to pursue her studies at polytechnic had been important in establishing a new identity. She had wanted to move away for this reason:

> There's five of us and I'm the youngest girl and me dad was always treating me like, you know, his baby girl, and I wanted to get out of it to show that I'm no longer his baby girl, so that was the main reason, I just wanted to leave home.

Since then her family relationships had improved:

> I feel as if I can talk to them about anything now, you know. I think he's (father) treating me a bit more as an adult now. So yeah, I think it's improved.

As part of her studies Laura had spent a year in Spain, working in the Madrid Chamber of Commerce, an experience which she felt had benefited her greatly. She had enjoyed her time there and felt that it had contributed to her self development, her sense of being "her own person":

> And then going to Spain's helped me even more and getting on and meeting new people from an entirely different culture.

Yet both her move to polytechnic, now one of the 'new Universities', at Sheffield, and her move to Spain had given her sharp reminders that she was a Liverpudlian:

> I never thought the North and South divide existed in England but it certainly does, and I only noticed that when I went away and met people from down south.

> People have got a bad attitude about Liverpool ... and once they know that you're from Liverpool, you know they do treat you differently, they do ... I thought I'm going to go to elocution lessons now because people, because of my accent they think I'm thick they do ... I mean even a woman from Southport phoned me once when I was in the Chamber and it was an English school over there that takes Spanish students and she said - Oh, I thought I recognised a common accent, are you from Liverpool? I mean that's a terrible thing to say to somebody you know.

Laura was trying to achieve an occupational transition at the same time as a social transition. Laura was a young woman of working class origins who had studied successfully and would 'probably be socially mobile' (interviewer's comment). Here, active transition behaviours were circumscribed by a sense of local identity and personal commitments as she felt tied to her native city by her fiancé and by her accent.

Tracy represents a case of someone who simply took the next step which presented itself and thereby obtained a job, but a job with no prospects. She lacked the self confidence to break away and try something new and was also trapped in her job by her commitment to her family and by the lack of opportunities on the local labour market. Her father was unemployed. Tracy's description of her own experience of finding a job is phrased in rather negative terms:

Interviewer: Was that (office work) what your YTS training prepared you for?

Tracy: Yeah

Interviewer: And was that what you always wanted to do?

Tracy: Yeah, the only thing I was any good at in school was English and typing, so it had to be something like that. So that's what I went in for.

Interviewer: It doesn't sound like a very positive choice. Was it just that you ruled out a lot of other things?

Tracy: Yeah, I didn't have anything specific in mind really. Then this came up and I just thought, oh well, I'll just do that really.

Tracy did not have a very positive view of herself or very much self-confidence. She dismissed an O level success, putting it down to chance.

> Government, Economics and Commerce. I don't know how I got it though, but I got it ... I think it was because I was the only girl in the class at the time.

She was uncertain about leaving Liverpool:

> I don't know what I'd do now ... I'm not sure what I'd do now if I wanted to leave Liverpool. I'm not sure where I'd go.

Tracy in fact had made an attempt to go to London, but it had ended unsuccessfully:

> I was going to move to London once, er me and me mate was going to see if we could get a better job and that, but mum got really upset about it and so we just ended up staying.

Tracy also found it difficult at times coping with her family's reactions to unemployment, and the emotional climate this created at home. Her father in particular she saw as often depressed about his own situation.

Above all she attached importance to security: staying in an unsatisfactory situation was preferable to taking any kind of risk:

> I'm scared to fail at something, instead of getting stuck without a job lined up, stick to what's secure.

Tracy also had a negative view of her school experiences:

> I never liked school that much actually. It was OK in the last few years but in the beginning I just couldn't wait to go into the seniors. I didn't like it all ... I didn't think what we were doing made that much sense really. I like I was never very good at maths anyway, but all they ever made you do was maths (sic) and I don't use it, I don't see the point of learning it.

She returned to the subject of negative reactions to accent and ways in which the Liverpool accent proved to be an impediment in the context of moving elsewhere, even to Manchester. She hinted at active animosity in the form of 'trouble':

> I don't think I'd go down very well in Manchester with a Liverpool accent ... No, I wouldn't stand much of a chance ... I can't open me mouth (in Manchester) otherwise there might be a bit of trouble. It's not very nice.

Tracy was a case of passive transition behaviour, lack of confidence in her own ability and achievements leading her to accept unsatisfactory situations rather than take the risks which might lift her out of them, but in which she might 'fail' and compound her own feelings of inadequacy.

Linda had been unemployed for fifteen months at the time of her interviews. She found it 'hard living on the dole, very hard'.

She had worked previously, and had obviously enjoyed the work because of the social contact:

> I want to work with people, I like working with people, I love being in a nice atmosphere like when I worked in McDonalds. I loved it because it was different people all the time.

Linda talked a lot about the financial difficulties of being unemployed. After giving her mother £15 a week she had little left to live on and had to save for some essentials such as shoes:

> After you buy your toiletries and say you need a new pair of shoes you've got to save that fifteen pounds till you get your next Giro and then like go out and buy a decent pair of shoes or a decent pair of trainers. I'm forever borrowing and paying back.

Linda, despite being unemployed and living in a 'rough' part of Liverpool, did seem to have a good deal of self-confidence and a positive self-image.

Talking about her school experience, she said:

> I just wanted to be treated like a grown up because I thought I acted like one. Like I was sensible, I was trustworthy, I was reliable, and that's how I felt I was about myself.

Occupational success is not of course the only factor in creating a positive self-image. Linda got on well with her mother and was living with her boyfriend in her mother's house:

> I can talk to my mum about anything whatsoever. I tell my mum everything.

> Oh yeah ... like I did lose me confidence until I started going out with my boyfriend and then like he said, well come on girl pick yourself up, you can do it, like all you've got to do is find the right job for yourself and you know you can do it.

Despite this, she appeared to be 'waiting for something to turn up' at the time of the interview rather than taking specific steps to change her situation. Linda appeared to be in a socially supportive working class family environment and spoke at some length about her school experiences and her attitudes to school. At her first secondary school she had been threatened with a knife by two sixth form girls and had left for another school. Here, she had found the behaviour of the boys difficult to cope with:

> ... And it was hard to concentrate 'cause they were all like babbling to you and they're messing around and the teacher's trying to talk to you, and you're trying to listen, but you can't 'cause they're throwing pens and flicking things and oh, its unbelievable, they're all horrors. I just don't know how they cope I don't know how the teachers cope. I could never be a teacher 'cause I'd be killing the kids. I've seen it and I've been one of the kids and I know what they're like. They're terrible, it's what people enjoy isn't it.

Linda associated school or college with authority and lack of autonomy, and would not consider returning for further study, for this reason:

> Authority! I hate authority, I hate being told what to do ... the thing about school is that they don't treat you like an adult.

Respondents with successful occupational transitions in view also sometimes expressed their school leaving as a kind of escape and breaking free. One told a story about his last day at school:

> Looking back I think it was good. I must admit, at the time I hated it, I think I'm like any kid that hated going to school ... the day I left I just got all my school books took them round and burned them with paraffin, and then that was it, burnt them so that I could see the back of that place. To be honest ...

> I'd have preferred to look back at my books now, but er that's one of them things I suppose.

William had a complex career, of a kind rather untypical for Liverpool. He had begun as an apprentice with a TV and video firm for two and a half years on leaving school. Eventually he gave up this job. As he had a driving licence he was used by the firm to deliver their products to customers, and he felt that he was simply not learning enough about the trade, particularly about repairing equipment. After two weeks unemployment he got a job in a factory through the job centre. This involved filling cans and bottles with cooking oil, and he found the job boring and unpleasant and left after two weeks. After another couple of weeks unemployment he went on an Employment Training course as a joiner, but had to leave because the 'sawdust gave him asthma'. Through a friend he had then obtained a job as an apprentice electrician and had just completed the first year of training. To have one formal apprenticeship, let alone two, is unusual in the British situation, and even in the depressed Liverpool labour market William was never unemployed for more than two weeks at a time.

William also was living with his parents, both of whom were unemployed, and who were supported financially by himself and his sister. He gave his parents twenty pounds per week. As they were living in a council house and he was gainfully employed he had the status of a lodger, and was therefore obliged to pay another thirteen pounds a week. In total he was paying out more than a third of his income, as an apprentice, to his parents.

> My Dad put pressure on us to study in the first place really, because he didn't, and he wants our lives to be different to his ... there was pressure to carry on with our education and not leave school at sixteen definitely, definitely.

William stated that his parents had left him to make his own decisions about a career. Nevertheless when he had been unemployed he had talked about the situation with his father:

> When I was on the dole for them two weeks, I was talking with me dad and he was saying you're better getting a trade behind you and they (sic) were talking to me about that.
>
> *Interviewer:* Did he have a trade behind him?
>
> *William* No he was working in the car factory ... but he said you're best learning something 'cause he's always worked in a factory he's got nothing to fall back on.
>
> *Interviewer:* So it's his experience that's made you want a trade?

William: Yeah, I just want a trade.

Interviewer: But apart from that do they direct you in any way?

William: No, it's up to me what I wanted to do. If I'd just done nothing they wouldn't have minded, as long as I'm happy they're happy.

If he had a problem, William said: 'If I've got to talk to somebody, maybe I'd talk to my girlfriend first, or maybe I'll talk to my mum and dad, but otherwise I just keep it to myself'.

When William left school he had obtained his first apprenticeship through the influence of his brother who was working for the firm. William's second apprenticeship he obtained through a personal contact:

> My mate got me this job then ... me friend, he works for this firm and he's our boss. He said are you looking for a job, gave it to me and I've been working there ever since like.

It is worth noting that the quality of this post appeared to be much better than anything William had been offered by the job centre or on his government Employment Training placement.

Structure and agency

Further light is shed on questions of structure, agency and the feelings of control or fatalism young people have about their transitions by group interviews with students aged sixteen to twenty experiencing various forms of vocational further education in Colleges of Further Education. The interviews were carried out at the time of the major 'Dearing' reviews of the mid-1990s. These are called the 'college sample'[1].

Gender issues featured prominently within group discussions, sometimes with little prompting by the interviewer. The following exchange took place in an all-female group:

Interviewer: Do you think there's any sexism in employment practices?

Natalie: I still do think there's a bit. There's bound to be some ... We're not really going to get rid of it. I think it's better now.

Susan: If it was say ... two male managers doing the same interview and there was ... a girl and a boy going for a job I think ... they would always go for the boy over the girl.

Natalie: It does depend on the job as well ... If it was a mostly male environment they would have gone for the man.

---

[1] These group interviews were carried out by Dr Peter Rudd, ESRC research student under supervision of the author, 1993-1996.

Susan [who is in the Business/Administration group]: Although you hardly get any male secretaries.

Natalie: Oh, you get quite a few now, you'd be surprised.

Susan: It's still considered as, like, a woman's job is a secretary.

Natalie: I mean a lot more men are becoming that now. Because if you think about it there's more jobs in there now than there are builders and bricklayers and that, so they have to turn their skills to something else.

Interviewer: Higher level jobs seem to be occupied by men, do you feel strongly about that?

Susan: Well, you go to work anywhere, you're virtually guaranteed that your boss will be a man.

Natalie: There's a new woman Chief Constable isn't there? She's got a top job, I saw that [on TV] last night. It is getting better gradually.

Elizabeth: It can only go slowly anyhow ...

Susan: I don't think now, oh women should be at home, you know, doing the cooking or anything. I don't think a lot of men can accept they've got a woman for a boss, because it's a bit sort of demeaning or whatever.

Interviewer: Does this ever affect any of you personally, on an individual level: you think 'I won't apply for that job because a female wouldn't get it'?

Natalie: No, I don't see why not. You should just apply for it anyway, whether it states male or female. They shouldn't do that because that's sex discrimination ... They're supposed to offer it to everyone ... Each should have equal opportunity to get the job.

Ethnicity also arose as a central issue where there was direct experience of its effects in the job market:

Serena: Each time I go into [a local supermarket where she had previously applied for a job] I see new people, English people, at the checkouts, I never see anyone like me.

Friendship networks and peer groups exerted strong influences. 96 per cent of the questionnaire sample indicated that they were 'satisfied' or 'very satisfied' with their friendships. Peers were sometimes influential in helping individuals to clarify the options open to them at the ages of 16 and 18. When the respondents were asked to give reasons for their particular choice of college and course, friends were often mentioned: 'I already knew people there' or 'my friend recommended the course' were typical comments.

Some of the interviewees remarked on the activities of friends who were not at the college and noted how peer pressures sometimes had to be resisted:

> *Susan*: Well I get a bit upset when I see all my friends driving around in their flashy cars and everything because they've been working since they were 16. And they say to me 'oh, when are you going to finally get a job?', you know. Just because they've got a job doesn't mean I have to go out and get one.

This applied particularly in the college sample in the labour market in which levels of direct entry into employment are considerably higher than the national average. It is not surprising that these college students experienced such peer pressures in this town, which illustrates how 'pull factors' operate in strong labour markets.

Individual effort and 'luck'

Well over half the respondents in each of the localities indicated viewed finding a job as 'very much down to the individual'.

An all-male discussion group drawn from the College samples particularly emphasised the importance of individual effort, along with an element of luck:

> *Interviewer:* How would you support your statement that [finding a job] is very much down to the individual? What do you mean by that?
>
> *John:* Given the effort you have put in, the confidence you have in yourself.
>
> *Wayne:* If you've got the qualifications, well I mean it is down to individual luck on the day, if you get a job.
>
> *John:* Put the effort in, put yourself out
>
> *Interviewer:* This question of 'luck' is quite interesting .....
>
> *Wayne:* Well, yeah. I've known [employing] organisations that have had a hat. They've got five or six people and pulled one out.
>
> *Interviewer:* Would you not accept that there are people who make the effort, get the qualifications and then don't get a job? Now why do you think that happens?
>
> *John:* Luck
>
> *Wayne:* Luck, again.

The notion of the college (and the family) providing guidance, but not taking over the decision-making responsibilities of the young people, is illustrated in the following interview comments:

Interviewer: How much of what you've done in the last couple of years has been your own decision, and how much of it has come from other people?

Phil: That is a very good question ....

John: I've had help from other people, like parents.

Interviewer: So you've taken their advice, but ultimately it's been your decision?

John: Yes

Wayne: I didn't .... I've just done what I wanted to do. Mind you, I was working anyway, so I mean, I didn't have to ask my mum or dad if I could do this or that.

Interviewer: Right, so in theory you've had control over choosing a course and going to college?

Wayne: Yeah, I just told them I was going to do it.

Interviewer (to the group): This word 'control', do you feel you've been in control, or do you feel sometimes you've been pushed perhaps by other people?

Russell: In control I'd say

Phil: In control. Just taking advice from parents and friends, but mainly in control

Russell: They give advice, but it's up to us. They're not going to push us.

Phil: They know they can't keep us in cotton wool for long, we've got to start learning our own ways, start being responsible.

Interviewer: Do you feel that attitude (of responsibility) has come from the college as well?

Phil: Yeah, like we're responsible for the work we do and we've got to meet deadlines and we've got to be responsible in how we set our work out and get it in on time.

Wayne: I mean it's not like at school where, you know, you're taken every step of the way ... you're told what you're going to do. I mean at college it's left up to you, whether you're going to achieve or not.

The overall impression, derived from all sets of data, is that the relationships between these students and their families tended to be based on support and encouragement, usually without too much pressure on the students to follow a particular pathway after college. Many young people expressed a view that while parents would often advise and encourage, they were not pushed in a particular direction and on the whole they were allowed the freedom to make their own decisions. Less than one-fifth of the young people in the college samples felt that family background was important when looking for a job. It would seem that families do have an influence, but often an indirect one: this suits the young people at a time when they are striving to establish their own adult identity and commensurate levels of independence. Support from the family is usually there if they need it, but at the same time most feel they are allowed the freedom to 'make their own way' to their educational and occupational destinations.

Overall, the data added up to a picture of family members and college personnel guiding, but not pushing, as perceived by the young people themselves. Several students suggested that they were aware of what was going on around them and that they would take advice if necessary, but ultimately they would take and be responsible for their own decisions: "We're not turning a blind eye to anything. We know what's happening, but we're also going our own way" (Rita).

What do these case studies of winners and losers in the transition process tell us?

The case studies over time illustrate how depressed labour markets shaped life experiences and chances in multiple and complex ways. They indicate a need to provide young people with a strong enough base to exercise a degree of independence from the vagaries of their local labour market. At present this is confined to those in the academic trajectories and some in well defined and supported apprenticeship routes.

As well as local labour market structures and conditions, the profiles illustrate how the shaping of trajectories reflects cultural capital. Support and guidance came from families and friends in the social network, and support and information services were most often used by higher achievers and those most advantageously positioned through family background and networks, as in the case of Stuart. When young people could identify 'careers advice', it was always of the information-giving kind, as this exchange illustrates:

> *Interviewer:* Have you ever been influenced by ... careers advisers in making your plans for the future?
>
> *Susan:* What careers advisers? [Group laughter]
>
> *Natalie*: My tutor helped me, on my first course I did, she said 'why don't you go for that one?
>
> *Interviewer:* Do you think they could have done more in terms of careers advice?

Natalie: Yeah

Susan: I mean, we used to get an hour a week, if that, talking about careers, but usually it was talking about like, all the boys wanted to talk about condoms. You know because we liked to talk about them in that lesson. Careers never really got a mention!

Natalie: Oh, yeah, we could have the advice leaflets, don't forget that!

Susan: Yeah, you could have a leaflet if you wanted one.

Natalie: ... telling you about secretarial jobs.,

Elizabeth: You had to find them yourself, sort of read through the whole pile to find what you want.

The challenge is to find ways of making support services and guidance less dependent on the cultural capital of the user, and to encourage proactive behaviours among those less well positioned. If individualisation is occurring in the experiences of young people there is a need to support active forms of transition behaviour. The experiences and career patterns represented in the 'case histories' (of which examples were given in the earlier part of this chapter), could be placed on a 'grid' (Figure 5.1). Their initial career trajectory is given in brackets.

While the cases are small in number and cannot be taken as representative, careful selection from a larger sample of cases with reference to initial trajectory and labour market together with problem-centred interviewing allows a picture to be built up of the ways young people perceive and act on their situation, and on their transitional biographies. Taken together the cases showed how step-by-step behaviours tended to accompany stagnant career patterns; 'wait and see' approaches characterised the 'losers' in transitions in downward drift patterns. There were examples of ways in which taking chances took young people out of their predicted trajectories. Features of the local labour market and support of the social networks available were part of the calculation of risk.

The cases selected from a wider set of biographical interviews show that there is no single transition, or single outcome and that young people are individuals with a degree of agency. They create their identities and meanings through complex processes of accommodation, resistance and negotiation of the social structures which surround them. Sometimes this involves 'active responses to social contradictions' a phrase used by Anyon (1983) in an analysis of gender identity development.

The cases illustrate differences in transition behaviours. They show us how transition behaviours reflect identities, which are themselves shaped by structures and localities. They show how structures speak via the subjectivities of the actors, and the identities they have assumed.

CAREER PATTERNS Transition Behaviour	PROGRESSIVE	UPWARD DRIFT AND REPAIRED	STAGNANT	DOWNWARD DRIFT
Strategic	Stuart *(Acad)* Cathy *(Acad)*	Brian *(Trans)*	Judy *(JobwTg)*	
Step-by-step		Jane *(JobwTg)*	Steve *(Acad)* John *(Acad)* Tracy *(TransEd)* Laura *(Acad)*	Graham *(VocEd)*
Taking chances/risks		Carol *(TransEd)* William *(JobwTg)* Malcolm *(Unemp)* Michael *(JobwTg)*		Anthony *(Unemp)*
Wait-and-see				Alan *(JobwTg)* Lynne *(Trans)* Angela *(Trans)* Linda *(Job)*

Full-time academic education = (Acad); Full-time vocational education = (VocEd); Direct job entry with training = (JobwTg); Direct job entry without training - (Job); Transitional, prevocational courses = (Trans); Unemployment/'schemes' = (Unempl).

Figure 5.1: Transition behaviour and career patterns

For example, narrowing of occupational horizons is shown both by those on privileged trajectories who consider no other options (Stuart, for example, and by those with limited prospects, who set their sights on what they believe is achievable for them, and judge their success or failure accordingly. Both judge themselves successful if they achieve that which they believe achievable for them, and feel themselves to be in control of that process.

Taken together these case studies have shown that:
a) The quality of education and training provision makes little difference if the labour market is depressed; structural influences are more important
b) Transition behaviour reflects both cultural capital and past experience, and plays its part in determining outcomes
c) Social networks play important parts in connecting young people into opportunity structures.

Without denying the structural foundations of transitions, it is the case that young adults are active agents in the construction of their identities and life chances. It has already been argued that one challenge is to educate broadly, to provide them with a strong enough foundation of knowledge and skill to maximise independence from the constraints and vagaries of local labour markets. Another challenge is to harness the belief that choices are possible and that actions, individual and collective, can influence outcomes in significant ways. This is not to compound young people's difficulties by 'making them believe they can resolve collective problems through individual action' as Furlong has argued. Proactive transition behaviours *together with sufficient social and educational support* are needed if individualisation is to go hand in hand with re-connection into the wider communities in which goals are pursued and choices made.

6 Competence and citizenship: which versions are required for times of critical social change?

Which versions of competence and citizenship are required for times of critical social change? The individual winners and losers in transition illustrate the interplay between structures and subjective experience. This chapter turns to accounts of the changing nature of work and the effects of social change on status passages. It moves beyond the broad metaphors of the dynamics of social change to the specifics of the social and material conditions which contribute to the shaping of learning and experience in early adult life. Which versions of citizenship and competence are required for these conditions and experiences of social change? How can these versions best be supported and achieved through education and wider social policies?

In all European countries, young adults are experiencing uncertain status and are dependent upon state and parental support for longer periods than would have been the case a generation ago. The case studies illustrate how, faced with changing opportunity structures, people have to find their own ways of reconciling personal aspirations with available opportunities and their own values in the domains of education, consumption, politics, work and family life. Achievement and recognition of adult status comes at different times in different spheres of life. The cases show how role and status become differentiated across the different domains of life and experience, and defining an individual as an adult and citizen may hinge on multiple roles performed. Young adults may be caught in disjunctions and contradictions of policies which do not recognise the interplay of the private and public domains and are based on invalid assumptions about common characteristics and needs of age ranges. As Jones and Wallace (1992) have pointed out, age-graded welfare entitlements in particular can lead to gross inequalities, with the recognition of varying domestic circumstances a 'missing ingredient' in the social security criteria of need. To understand transitions to adult, worker and citizen status, we also have to understand the 'private world of family life' (p. 69). Andruske (1997), for example, demonstrates the 'forgotten citizenships' of reciprocity and rights of difference when the entire focus is on legitimation of individuals' citizenship through paid labour, by focusing on the situation of 'mothers on welfare' and the effects of 'welfare to work' policies on these young women and their families.

Social changes in the inter-related domains of work, education, family and community all affect transition behaviours, which themselves reflect personal identities and aspirations as well as the opportunity structures with which young adults are faced. According to Baethge (1989), the processes of individualisation of the life course are increasing inconsistencies and ambiguities in the status of young adults. Inconsistencies need to be identified and addressed if policies are to maximise means of achieving active, responsible and fulfilling participation in society, through full citizenship.

Work and status passages

Individualisation is linked with emerging post-Fordist scenarios in the organisation of work, where the scene is set for social control via increased surveillance (Ball, 1990) or creation of new possibilities for social transformation, with education as the engine for change (Brown and Lauder, 1992).

In the work arena, transitions to worker status are defined by institutionalised rules concerning recognised qualifications and credentials. These credentials testify to the knowledge, competence and experience of the holder and their acquisition and application depend on the way in which the various credentials and selection systems are negotiated (Raffe 1991, Ainley 1994). This in turn is heavily influenced by cultural capital, particularly in respect of access to information, advice, social support and personal networks. Young adults bring different transition behaviours to these situations, and success in negotiating these structure and networks can bring stability or instability to the life course. For those who are unsuccessful in gaining entry to jobs, long term unemployment cuts young adults off from the opportunities of the market, from access to work-based credentialling systems and from the exercise of citizenship in any significant sense (Evans and Heinz 1994).

Even successful entry to the labour market can bring another set of limitations and instabilities. Early work entry can create premature foreclosure of options and stereotyped work identities. The Crowther Report (1959) described workplaces as deadening to the minds of young school leavers. Post-Fordist discourses now talk of 'learning organisations'. Post-Fordist discourses about the social and economic future attempt to normalise a view of the social organisation of work and present as inevitable what is in fact contingent and subject to political process (Edwards 1993). The post-Fordist scenario presented by writers such as Brown and Lauder (1982) is one of work transformed by new technology. Multi-skilled workforces need high levels of training underpinned by extended initial education which in turn acts as the driving force for wider social transformations and democratisation. The alternative version of this scenario presented by Edwards (1993) is one in which the disappearance of intermediate level jobs will leave a stratum of jobs demanding high levels of intellectual skill, competence and flexibility and a large mobile sector of casualised labour at all skill levels, operating by selling their services by contract. For those in the increasing ranks of casualised labour, narrow competences are unlikely to be of any use over time and members of a casualised pool of labour kept in on-going insecurity and instability are also unlikely to be able to engage in full participation in society in the sense implied in the maximal definitions of citizenship discussed earlier.

How has the changing employment situation of the 80s and 90s affected young people's attitudes to work? For some time, there was a version of the 'moral panic' over the effects of unemployment on young people's motivations to work. The traditional incentives of 'get good qualifications and get a good job' for the majority of school leavers could not be invoked by teachers, and fears that a generation would be raised lacking the 'work-ethic' were expressed in the early 1980s. In fact, the decline of employment opportunities for young people 'tightened the bonds' between education and employment in a host of ways. The 16-19 Initiative research carried out between 1987 and 1991 studied work and training attitudes, and showed that the value young people attached to training reflected whether or not it led to a proper job. Motivation to train is driven by the hope and expectations of work and it is evaluated accordingly. As Raffe (1991) has put it, education for its own sake is fair enough but training for its own sake is a contradiction in terms. Economic locus of control measures showed that high internal locus of control, or belief in one's influence and control over events, was associated with success both in education and in direct entry to work. These were also associated with political and social beliefs and often reflected more deeply held values. Work commitment was strong, with only a quarter of respondents disagreeing with the statement that 'having almost any job is better than being unemployed'; but a majority also agreed that 'you do not have to have a job to be a full member of society and that a job is not essential to life satisfaction'. Those closest to the labour market, and in jobs, had the strongest work commitment.

To what extent did these findings in the early '90s indicate a shift towards post-materialist values in work? When young adults were asked to select the three work characteristics they felt to be most important, a friendly atmosphere at work was chosen by two-thirds of all respondents, supporting the position that work is more than a means to an end for many young adults, who increasingly seek to develop personal identities and relationships through their work as well as life outside work. While non-materialistic considerations were rated highly by all groups, the most disadvantaged young people on the unemployed/under-employed trajectory saw career security and wages as very important. These, of course, were the very aspects of work denied them, and through lack of these other aspects of social life were affected. Academic young people, by contrast, balanced the social and quality aspects of work alongside the material. Attitudes to work are thus strongly affected by social location and experience of the labour market, with materialistic values strongest amongst those most adversely affected by depressed labour market conditions.

All of these findings are significant in the emergence of a casualised workforce. Strong internal locus of control will enable people to play the available labour market opportunities better than those with fatalistic attitudes. Training will not be valued and skills and motivation will not be sustained unless there are successful outcomes. The 'revolving door' approaches to training and labour market entry aim to maintain work commitment and instrumental work values amongst those most disadvantaged and most marginalised in work opportunities. But casualisation and the growth of the proportion of workers in relatively insecure jobs in small and medium companies which do not provide continuity of employment, let alone career progression and do not, by themselves, have a capacity for quality training, mean that there is a danger of skills loss and reinforcement of the low skills equilibrium which characterises the British labour market (Finegold and Soskice, 1990).

There may also be a lack of continuity in social identity construction. One of the major challenges is to provide for continuous development of knowledge-based skill for individuals with an emphasis on work identities, gained through skill ownership, recognition and membership of defined 'communities of practice' (Lave and Weiger 1991, Brown 1995). A second challenge is to provide a modernised framework of social support to ensure access to social citizenship for all, to counter diminishing entitlement and the slippery slope of making citizen rights dependent on worker status.

Education and status passages

The expansion of education which has been outlined in Chapter 3 has produced a new set of structures and experiences between the end of the compulsory phase of schooling at 16 and first entry to the labour market, at ages up to the mid-twenties.

The Anglo-German studies showed how far the developments in Britain in post-compulsory education have moved towards the 'workplace as curriculum authority' in introducing experiences related to the work place into educational settings. Many more young Britons agreed that they have been given responsibility, have been able to make decisions and use initiative and have developed other work-related competences than did young Germans at the same age (Chapter 3, Figure 3.6). Only in the categories 'developed new skills and abilities' and 'felt all abilities were being used', were the results similar. Some care has to be taken in interpreting these findings as young people in Britain are much closer to the labour market chronologically than their German counterparts, entering work at least two years ahead in all trajectories. The anticipation of work was therefore much nearer to their interests and concerns. The results also indicate that British provision is richer in these respects, perhaps making up for the lack of progression of opportunities subsequently. In Germany young people valued the experiences they were getting because of the general labour market utility of the credentials they were gaining. This is a marked example of *earning* the right to take responsibility rather than *learning* it through the educational process. In England, the approach was much more to surround young people with a range of work-related opportunities for learning, with the opportunities for progressing from learning into work much more haphazard and risky. There is also a prolonged dependency associated with extended post-compulsory education, which runs counter to the deeply embedded cultural values and expectations of a significant proportion of the working class population, particularly among males. While access to education is a right of social citizenship, in the post-compulsory phase this has become associated with decreased social citizenship rights in other areas, associated with increased dependency and assumptions of family support.

Families

Families can impede or support the transitions of early adulthood. For many young adults the experience of physical separation from the family for extended periods may result in improved understanding and appreciation and is part of the process of negotiating independence, as Banks et al (1992) have shown. For others, escape from the parental home is seen as the only way to achieve a sense of self and to exercise their own choices, however restricted these may be in reality. For some young adults thrown back into involuntary dependence on family through welfare policies, prospects for achievement of independence and citizenship may be impaired. It can be argued further that it should be a basic social right not to 'have to rely' on their family because alternatives do not exist (Finch 1995).

In the context of social changes and individualised transitions, the parental role becomes even more one of support rather than guidance. Few parents have experience of the options facing their children because of the pace of change in all aspects of work and education.

This is an arena in which status inconsistencies for young people are most pronounced. Jones and Wallace (1992) identified the 'basic ambiguity':

> Emancipation and citizenship status derive from economic independence, but some recognition of emancipation and access to some citizenship rights are required for the achievement of economic independence. This creates a 'double-bind' to which many young people are subject as they become older (p 92)

The 'double-bind' occurs because young adults are expected to become emancipated and independent - 'to stand on their own feet' - and one of the roles of the family is to assist in this process. The economic dimension is important here. When young people have a degree of financial independence - an independent source of income - their progress towards emancipation is enhanced. They become less subject to parental control and more able to exercise rights both inside and outside the home. Policies have progressively increased financial dependence of young people on their parents in the 16-18 age range, as access to unemployment benefit has been removed and training rates have assumed parental support. While the case for this can be argued for young people under the age of legal majority, that is the age of legal and political citizenship, after the age of 18 and up to the mid-twenties an assumption is made of financial dependency in the withholding of full adult rates of social security. What are the effects and implications of this?

The inter-connections between the three main transitions of the youth phase become significant here, as Coles (1996) has argued:

- Education, training and labour market careers
- Domestic careers (from families of origin to families of destination)
- Housing careers (from living dependent on families to living independently of them).

Often the transition involving education, training and entry to the labour market drives the other two transitions. For example, young people who follow the academic trajectory and live away from home while studying have moved to a form of 'half-way house'. These intermediate households form an important and recognised part of the transition process. For others 'intermediate households' are more risky. These involve staying in hostels or with friends. These carry a risk of moving onto homelessness, particularly where a welcome is outstayed or a 'fixed term' of stay expires, with lack of economic means through unemployment the major contributory factors.

More generally, for what reasons and under what circumstances do young people leave home? How does this link with early school leaving and with the increase in homelessness?

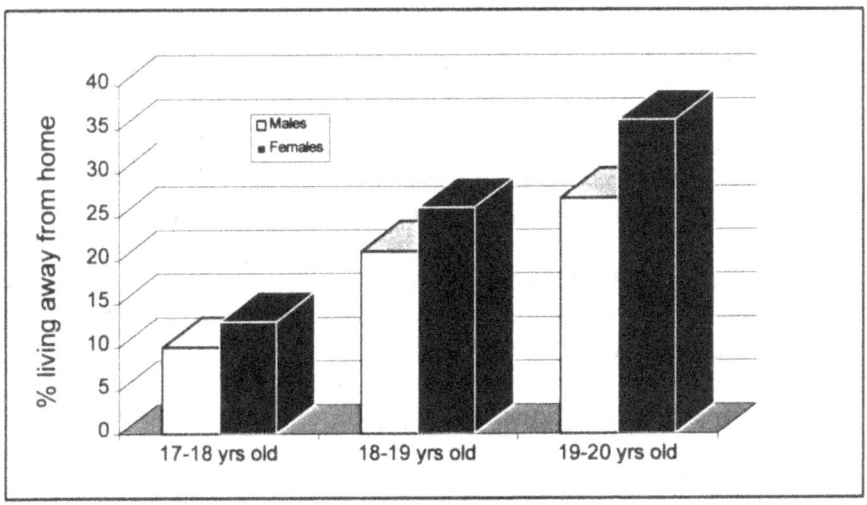

Figure 6.1: Percentages living away from home, by age

The 16-19 Initiative showed that, by the age of 19, most young people expressed a preference to live away from their families (Figure 6.1). Many young people go through a period of moving backwards and forwards between their parental home and intermediate housing before moving finally to the independent home. The statistics showed that more than 35 per cent of females aged 19-20 had left home, compared with 27 per cent of males. Ten percent of 15-16 year olds males and 11 per cent of females had left home. Leaving home earlier was not a problem in itself. It is leaving home prematurely which is problematic, when the young person does not have the means for independent living but 'push' or 'pull' factors operate. 'Push' factors are often associated with poor family circumstances and relationships while 'pull' factors are hopes of jobs in some distant and more promising labour market. Lack of access to affordable housing and unemployment are the major underlying causes of the drift into homelessness, where this occurs, and early leavers, who are at most risk of unemployment, are the most vulnerable. By 1997, up to 300,000 young people were experiencing homelessness each year (Justice, 1997).

Among samples of young people studied in the contrasting labour markets of Swindon and Liverpool, most young people were still living at home, receiving financial and other forms of support from their parents, as well as accommodation (Evans and Heinz, 1994). Young people in Swindon had a higher proportion of fathers in full-time employment (more than 90 per cent); compared with three-quarters in Liverpool. One in three mothers in Swindon were in full-time jobs, and one in four in Liverpool. Young people generally recorded a high degree of satisfaction with family life, and issues likely to cause arguments did not produce deep-seated dissatisfaction and conflict. The most likely source of arguments was help given or not given with domestic tasks in the home, with more than half reporting frequent arguments over this. One in five reported family arguments over the young person's occupational plans, particularly those on the 'lower' trajectories of semi-skilled or unskilled situations. Friends were also a cause of family arguments for one in five young people. One fifth were dissatisfied with their financial circumstances. Most young people reported that they were satisfied with their future prospects, irrespective of local economic conditions.

One in six of the Swindon respondents were living away from home, where the labour market provided better opportunities for early economic independence. More young people in the academic trajectories and unemployment/underemployment trajectories had moved away from home. Those on skilled and semi-skilled transitional work trajectories tended to remain at home for longer. In the academic trajectory, the higher level of leaving home reflected 'going away to University'. In the unemployed/ underemployed trajectory the higher moving out rate was associated with family pressures and bad housing conditions (push factors) and the pull factors of relatively buoyant labour markets. Two fifths of Swindon respondents and one-third of Liverpool expected to move to find work. There was also a higher tendency for girls to leave home early.

Policies are encouraging lengthening dependency both by increasing retention in education and training and by assuming parental support. Those for whom the push factors are irresistible, through family breakdown, for example, will be at greater risk of social exclusion and homelessness than previously, since policies are geared to retention. The policies will reduce numbers going into intermediate housing. For those who do go into intermediate housing (other than student housing) there is little incentive to continue in education and training unless financial support and affordable rents are available. The requirement to be available for work prevents participation in learning opportunities over a specified number of hours while on benefit, although there are moves to reduce this disincentive through New Deal and related initiatives. Parental support is assumed in the low level of training allowances, which do not cover accommodation and basic living costs.

The thrust of social policy to 'push young people back on families' can increase pressures on the family, both financial and personal, and is reflected in rising homelessness figures as young people leave or are pushed out without the 'social scaffolding' to support them.

In Germany, different cultural norms apply concerning dependency and age of accession to adult status. Young people are not expected to be earning until their 20s, there is not the same pull of the labour market and strong institutional structures allow for a degree of experimentation, false starts, and provide 'safety net' financial support for those for whom family support is not available. The wage packet as a symbol of growing up, so strong in Britain, does not hold to the same degree in Germany.

In the less institutionalised, less supportive British context, young people need help to break out of the vicious circles operating, but the circles themselves need to be tackled.

Social identities, status passages and community participation

Young adults participate in their communities in a number of ways. As well as being producers at work, they are consumers and they have a right to participate in the life of their local communities as citizens and voters. Fragmentation and diversification of the opportunity structure are combined with the effects of globalisation in which people increasingly become disassociated from their traditional contexts. This means that the search for identity or sense of wholeness and continuity as a person, gains a new intensity (Baethge 1989). Intergenerational transmission of 'virtues' is reduced, and the channels to participation in political and social structures may become obscured. Engagement in citizenship in its maximal sense is thus made more difficult, and the pursuit of 'ego-driven' projects may become paramount, as young adults act to maximise personal opportunity and reduce risk.

Many of these 'choices' are rooted in partly formed social identities, the senses young people have of who they are and what their capabilities are. Self definition involves internalising the definitions and attributes ascribed by others. These subjective identities are associated with social class, gender, race. They also reflect educational credentials and other mediating factors associated with experiences in the labour market and wider social context, with narrowing career options playing a part in shaping identities over time. While the latter are increasing in relative significance as traditional transition patterns become 'fractured' and extended, disadvantage continues to be concentrated in groups defined by class, gender and race in particular localities, as the 16-19 Initiative demonstrated. Social identities are reflected in social attitudes. These have been shown to be organised around institutionalised authority, gender and race, employment commitment and fatalism (Banks et al 1992), with the more 'political' dimensions of identity less sharply focused and less consistently expressed over time.

Interest in Politics

Only a minority of young people express any interest in politics and the level of interest appears to be waning. The British Social Attitudes Survey (Park, 1996) showed that the level of interest of 18-24 year-olds was significantly lower in 1994 than in 1991. Young people are influenced by national cultures, local communities and their experiences of success and failure during their transitions into adult life in their responses to politics and politicians. Many young people have low opinions of political parties and politicians generally. Their attitudes are not organised around political positions but around the 'politics of the personal' and wider political issues. The Anglo-German samples showed that strong feelings about education, housing and environmental issues could co-exist with the lack of interest they expressed in party politics. The overriding view was that young adults have been badly treated by national governments in the arenas of jobs, housing and education and training. They felt they were being given too little in return for the contributions they were expected to make to their societies. This applied irrespective of area and context.

Changes in political involvements between 16 and 20 are incremental. Very few young people develop any serious involvement in politics of the conventional kind. Changes in early adult life involve gradual increases in interest in political issues particularly among those who continue in education (Evans and Heinz 1994, Park 1996). The structures for democratic experience exist in many community groups yet youth participation in these, in so far as it is quantified, appears small.

Local organisations provide a means by which people engage with public life. They featured in the proposals for the Active Society (1969) that aimed to encourage young people's active and critical participation through the vehicles of Youth and Community work. Freire (1974) argued that

> People could learn social and political responsibility only by experiencing that responsibility, through intervention in the destiny of their children's schools, in the destinies of their trade unions and places of employment.... ...through associations, clubs and councils, and in the life of their neighbourhoods, churches and rural communities by actively participating in associations, clubs and charitable societies'

The approaches of the 'Learning by Participation' projects of the 1980s (Dalin, 1984) aimed to harness both work and wider community experience in these ways, to assist young people in their status passages.

However, as Mac-an-Ghaill (1996) argues, such approaches must address the conditions that fundamentally affect working class students' experiences of transitions into adult life:

> We need to incorporate a more dynamic perspective that sees schools as well as *reproducing* wider class divisions, also locally *producing* a range of class-based identities, involving complete social and psychic investments, that students and teachers come to occupy and live out. (p.172)

Yet the signs are that the media and advertising are creating alternative ways of establishing collective identities and a sense of belonging, often around consumer goods, trade names and symbols, with Nike trainers being the obvious example. This is significant, given that consumerism is an arena in which citizenship rights are being redefined. Williamson (1996) asks 'whether citizenship is anything more than a rhetorical device when it has been reduced to consumerism and when the social scaffolding which supported it has been dismantled?' (p.11).

The communitarian movement, as articulated by Etzioni (1995), puts forward self help, family support and community support as means to reconnect people at local level. As employment status and consumer power increasingly determine citizen status and rights, there is a fundamental problem of motivation to be addressed in the communitarian movement, among those disadvantaged in and by the operation of labour and consumer markets. As Williamson (1996, p.11) asks:

> There remain questions concerning the relationships between 'status' issues and issues of volition and competence. Where is young people's motivation to develop the latter, if the former are being systematically eroded?

Maximal versions required

Many factors can combine to marginalise and exclude young people. As citizenship became increasingly equated with consumer power under the politics of the 'new right', what was the position of young people unable to gain a foothold in work? Unemployment, which continues to fall disproportionately on those aged under 25, not only cuts young people off from work, but also from exercising consumer power in their leisure time. Adults' monopolies on local politics and democratic structures may also make it difficult for young people to participate and studies such as the 16-19 Initiative found widespread apathy, with the most politically alienated also likely to be the most politically impotent. But these studies have also shown keen interest in issues such as equality of opportunity and the environment and particular receptivity to changes in lifestyles and values.

Minimal versions of competence and citizenship are inadequate to deal with the social dynamics of the time, and young people's responses to them, since they neither equip with critical skills nor cultivate the sense of shared autonomy, in the broader context within which 'individual projects' are pursued.

Maximal approaches to the development of competence and citizenship have these processes at their centre. Interventions in shaping lives through education and social support are based on respect for individual autonomy.

They promote capability to make informed and independent judgements about courses of action and encourage participation in what Habermas (1970, 1976) has called 'communicative action', recognising the need for young people to be interactive in 'person-environment' relations particularly among peers. The person-environment relations in question link identity formation with context. Age cohort, gender, region, ethnicity and social class are contexts within which experience is gained and identities are formed. Family, peers, educational institutions and workplaces are agents in this process, shaping young people's subjective emotional experiences of support and satisfaction, their future expectations reflecting optimism or pessimism and their feelings of control in relation to norms and external expectations - their own experience of 'agency'. The social interactions which are necessary to develop competences and capacities for action are enhanced or impeded by social structures which either present structural barriers or create the potential for personal competences to 'unfold' under particular societal conditions. Communicative competence or 'undominated verbal discourse' amongst peers and equals is seen as an essential ingredient for this unfolding of competences. So also is mutual aid. In maximal approaches the educator may exercise *influence* through providing information, discussion of courses of action and their possible consequences, and creating conditions for the exercise of real responsibility and for exposure to different points of view. Smith (1992) labels this 'mutual aid' in which group control, collective achievement and person-centredness are emphasised over educator control, individual achievement and organisation-centredness.

All of these forms of intervention potentially create the conditions for attitude change, personality development and growing capability for participation and action. But the difficulties should not be under-estimated.

Two quotes from a research study carried out by a youth work practitioner and postgraduate research student Judith Jenner[1] (1994, p 131) illustrate the challenges these forms of practice present.

> The dominance of 'power over' as a means of exerting control was a direct contradiction of empowerment, a term used often in youth work philosophy. Encouraging a young person to have control over their own lives and be responsible for making their own decisions was for many in direct opposition to their experience of being controlled by others. This was not only the case in the wider community, but also within the young people's group.

The researcher also observed that participation could not be a reality when the power structures within the group itself were based on certain accepted group norms:

> When power was expressed in aggression and violence, gender differences or territorial claims, the powerless were not offered many choices. When young people participate and use power as control over others the system remains unchanged as the few will dominate the rest of the group. If there is to be equal participation then careful interventions have to be made by the worker. The dominant culture of the group may make it inappropriate to expect the group to work in a participative way.

This study produced an initial model of intervention (Figure 6.2), which may be made by adults or indeed peers, showing how three 'modes' of power are linked with different types of intervention and outcome. Thus control as a mode of power is linked with confrontation, use of gender roles and territory, producing disempowerment. Self determination uses strategies of experimentation, equal opportunities and sharing of ideas, producing empowerment and participation. Education, in this model, uses interventions of negotiation, information and equality of status as learners to bring about attitude change.

---

[1] Judith Jenner carried out the ethnographic study of Power: Participation or Control in Youth Work Practice under the supervision of Karen Evans and Shane Blackman at the University of Surrey.

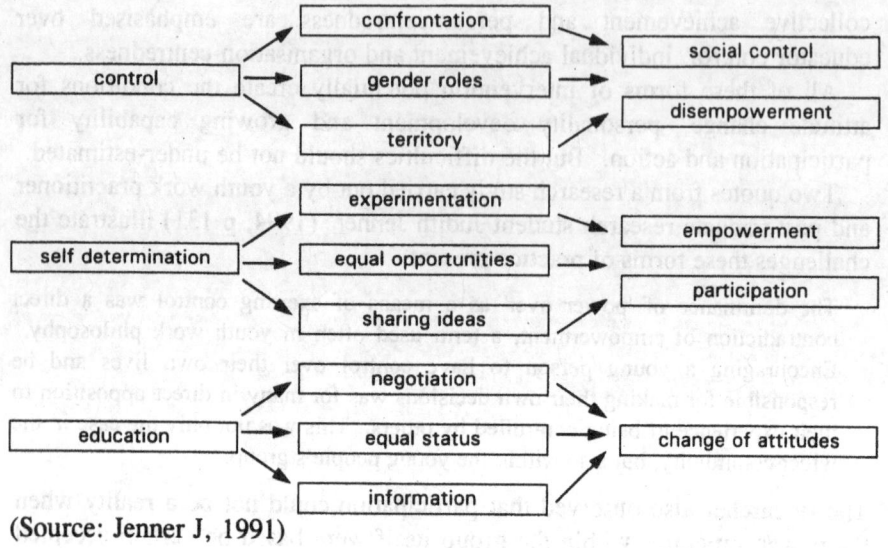

(Source: Jenner J, 1991)

Figure 6.2: Modes of power interventions and outcomes

Each individual needs to balance and manage 'internal and external realities', (Hurrelmann, 1988) that is their felt needs in relation to the environment in which they operate. Where there is a mismatch between felt needs and the opportunities the environment can provide, dissatisfaction results. Expectations may be 'unrealistic' because they stem from inadequate self concept and identity formation or they may be unrealistic because the immediate environment is overly constrained or hostile and the expectations could be better met by changing aspects of the environment. Individuals may accommodate or resist aspects of the social world, the structural influences around them. They may do so individually or collectively. Individuals need to be constantly regulating their behaviour and expectations in relation to the environment, while maintaining and developing a values base, which gives meaning to goals and actions. They need to become 'productive processors of reality' in Hurrelmann's terms, goal directed in their behaviour, with the capacities to regulate and adjust their actions, achieve and redefine goals and boundaries and to participate in change.

In this sense, they are engaged in the transformation of experience into knowledge and action, the foundations of experiential learning, which emphasises the process of adaptation and learning over content or specific outcomes. These processes lie at the heart of maximal approaches to learning for competence and citizenship, when set in a modernised framework of material and social support. Figure 6.2 summarises the variables which are significant in shaping the course of lives, producing different levels of economic and political engagement, allied to personal goals.

Structural Variables	Intervening Variables (socialisation conditions)	Psycho-Social Processes	Person-Environment Behaviours/ Actions	Outcomes
• Gender	• Family	• Identity formation	• Active	• Political participation
• Social Class	• Peers			
	• Media			
• Ethnicity	• Social networks		• Passive	
	• Resources	• Self concept and esteem		
• Labour Market	• Locality			• Economic participation
	• Educational institutions		• Accommodating	
↓	• Educational qualifications			
♦ Structural and Ascribed Attributes	• Credentials		• Resistant	• Personal goals
	↓			
	♦ Acquired Attributes			

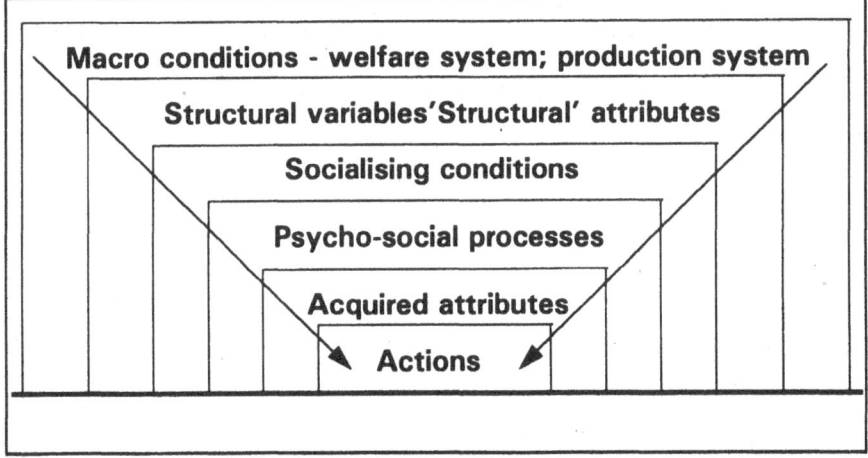

Figure 6.3: Variables influencing transition behaviours and outcomes

Interventions in processes, actions and outcomes (Figure 6.2) can draw on resources from all parts of the community, involving a range of providers working in partnership to produce co-ordinated strategies which can extend individual capacities while, at the same time, adapting the more hostile features of the environment which can defeat and ultimately exclude.

Person-centred approaches must be combined with altering the material and social environment so that demands do not become so great that young people cannot cope unaided. When demands exceed capacity to cope, social citizenship is eroded and social exclusion results for many. The *conditions* for social inclusion and participation must be created and sustained, if we are to avoid the pitfalls and contradictions of one-sided approaches which imply that individual action and competence can solve societal and structural problems which are collectively encountered (Furlong 1997).

Thus measures must aim to:
i. *Encourage active transition behaviours by* problem-solving behaviours, developing 'action competences', encouraging self-managed learning and understanding of self in relation to others;

ii. *Make the social/material environment less hostile to those most at risk of exclusion, through*
   - social support;
   - targeted help and guidance;
   - financial support and entitlements for study;
   - access to affordable housing.

All of this rests, fundamentally, on motivation to participate, which itself springs from the overall senses of purpose and meaning felt in individual lives. If motivation is lacking on a large scale, how can purpose and meaning be restored?

7 Back to the future: from transferable skills to educated attributes

The transformations of the time require a renewed valuing of and commitment to learning: as the boundaries between languages and cultures begin to dissolve, as new skills and knowledge are expected within the world of work and, most significantly, as a new generation, rejecting passivity in favour of more active participation, needs to be encouraged to exercise such qualities of discourse in the public domain.

(Stewart Ranson, 1994)

In considering the future role of education and training in promoting citizenship and competence in this global scenario of change, Pallas (1993) has alerted us to the dangers of limiting our sights to one country, since doing so 'removes from view two key factors that shape the life course of individuals: institutional arrangements and culture' (p.430). Chapters 5 and 6 have shown that there is a need to consider how the roles of student and trainee are connected with the other roles young adults play in their early careers. Analysis of how these interconnect in different cultural contexts provides further insights into the factors which may be significant in framing future policies.

Super and Sverko (1995), for example, show how different cultural values affect the importance attached to different life roles. They found a 'dominant' value pattern in North America, for example, of upward mobility, material success and prestige, with much higher importance attached to 'work' and 'home-making' roles than to other roles such as that of 'student'. This contrasted with the European tendency towards higher valuation of relationships and understanding, autonomous life styles, coupled with strong rejection of authority and relatively more emphasis on the importance of studying. These studies, based on 'work importance' measures applied internationally, also recognised marked differences within and between cultural and sub-cultural groupings. Interestingly, the 'citizen' role was not generally deemed to start until the age of 20, and was associated strongly with community activities.

Chisholm's study (1991) of youth and social policy in the EC Member States showed that policy in general displayed 'little grasp of young people's contemporary situation, and the relationships between schooling and socio-economic change', citing as an example Spanish experience as reflected in a paper submitted to the EU Research into Youth Matters Group:

> Youth is a factor in the process of social modernisation. Since the 1960s, the traditional ways in which generations pass through a sequence of roles and statuses have been gradually silting up. Today, there is a discrepancy between that which is taught (in the schools) and that which will be necessary for life tomorrow. (p.70)

Other countries, notably in Scandinavia, see their schooling provision as open, flexible and strongly future oriented, complemented by strong associative life through which most young people regularly spend time participating in group activities:

> Where competition and individual achievement do not play a significant role, they can more readily develop a sense of positive self-worth. (p.70)

This is part of a wider commitment to 'socially-engaged integration', a policy which had begun to run into problems in Denmark in the early 1990s as over-institutionalisation of organised cultural life lost touch with the values of young people themselves.

For Member States of the European Union that did have an explicit youth policy citizenship was identified as 'the anchoring concept which informs its nature and purpose'. Dutch youth policy for example considers all children and young people as citizens in their own right from birth, with policies and services designed to support and protect young citizens in their different phases of development towards adulthood (Chisholm, 1991) while French policies emphasise future-oriented citizenship education, based on acquisition of skills of analysis, reflection and action, aspirations for social justice and 'mutual solidarity' between young people and the rest of society.

Developing workers and citizens: two national models compared

Throughout this volume, reference has been made to Anglo-German studies (Bynner and Roberts 1991; Evans and Heinz 1994; Evans, Behrens and Kaluza 1998) in which comparisons have been made of the ways in which young adults achieve worker and citizen status in Britain and Germany. Analysis of the ways in which these transitions are structured and supported gives further insights into maximal and minimal approaches, as experienced by matched samples of young adults aged 17-22.

In Britain, transition structures are weakly institutionalised, and post-compulsory education and training arrangements reflect historically embedded narrowness and divisions, with the 'elite' Advanced level and the narrowly based National Vocational Qualifications exemplifying the academic/vocational divide. Chapters 1 to 3 discussed ways in which the curriculum has been progressively shaped by instrumental values and the presumed needs of employers. In particular, the NVQ system is predicated on minimalist notions of competence based performance, which are of questionable relevance to future skill needs and are outdated quickly. Not only do they fail to develop the broad-based underlying capabilities appropriate to the social dynamics of the time (Skilbeck, 1986) but they are also highly individualistic, reinforce structural inequalities and run counter to the development of interdependence (Blackman and Evans, 1994). Criticisms of narrowness are offset by post-hoc attempts to broaden the curriculum by 'entitlements' and 'transferable skills' which occupy an ambiguous and weak place in the curriculum, and are not comparable in breadth or depth to the general education provided at this stage in many European countries.

In Germany strongly institutionalised transition structures post-16 provide broadly based foundation training designed to produce educated workers and citizens. Young adults are further removed and protected from early experiences in the 'market' as producers and consumers than British young people. Longer periods of preparation combined with access to widely recognised credentials make young adults more independent of local labour markets. Building on the foundations established by Kerschensteiner, participation in the Berufsschule (colleges providing part-time education as an adjunct to firm-based training within the dual system) continues to be compulsory for all German young people up to the age of 18 if they are not in full-time education or training. It is expected by young people and parents that education will continue for all until 18. The Berufsschule has a clear role in continuing general education embracing the humanities and foreign languages as well as supporting the vocational aspects of apprenticeships in partnership with employers. The community holds high expectations of trainees in Germany. As one head of Berufsschule observed, 'people expect an educated citizen and it is therefore a mistake to think that political education is not necessary'. The expectation is that 'every student will learn continuously throughout his or her life'.

This is not to minimise problems of the German system identified through the Anglo-German studies and discussed elsewhere (Brown and

Evans 1994). While the commitment to continued general education within apprenticeship aligns conceptually with development of citizenship through liberal education, in practice the experience is often poor in pedagogical terms, involving repetition of previous studies in ways which, as reported by students, do little to encourage engagement with the subject matter, let alone critical reflection upon it (Evans and Heinz, 1994). The dual system in Germany also gives a degree of employer control which tends to reproduce rather than counter structural disadvantages, manifested in the differentials of value and quality ascribed to typically 'male' or 'female' apprenticeships (Bynner, 1994). There is however a strong corporatist strand with an assumption of common purpose and co-determination between the 'social partners' on both sides of industry. It provides credentials which are accepted as indicators of generic competence and have wide labour market utility. Instead of addressing changing requirements of work through narrow competences, recent developments are emphasising problem-solving and team working as more effective future-oriented means of dealing with change (Brown et al, 1994).

In England, leaving education at 16 used to mark the change of status from 'school kid' to adult with all the accoutrements of money, status and independence that this implied. Failure to achieve it, which was the lot of the great majority of leavers, bred a frustration with the situation and endless seeking of new opportunities to change it. The institutions of the wider English society treat most school leavers as near-adults. Banks and building societies are prepared to lend money to young people in the form of mortgages, credit cards and overdrafts. In Germany awarding credit to people who are not seen as fully responsible citizens is rare and if it occurs at all always involves a large deposit. Dependency status is assumed and expected by everybody until the early to mid-twenties and there is, in consequence, far less frustration with low financial status among German young people.

Difficult family situations and lack of financial resources pose a serious threat to prospects in many instances. In Germany because of the assumed dependency status over a longer period and financial support systems for those young people whose families cannot support them, young people are enabled to keep their options open for much longer. The system protects them against their difficulties. Nevertheless, for some, what is on offer is insufficient to keep them in the VET system, and a downward drift into marginal employment becomes inevitable. The problem has now become compounded in Germany where the new Länder of the former East Germany face great problems in offering VET provision which is comparable to that taken for granted in the former West Germany[1]. In England the preferred response to all difficult financial and family situations has traditionally been to terminate education and seek a job. In England young adults are much closer to the labour market than their German counterparts, and enter it at least two years earlier, so in many respects the range of work attributes they have acquired in their early careers is wider than in Germany. Many young people who *have* continued in further education emphasise that they want choices within an *all-round* education, with a curriculum that includes the relevant technical skills, alongside personal and social development, and emphasises learning processes as well as outcomes. While the narrowness of curriculum content for many users of Further Education colleges is a weakness, the *processes* and *climate* of learning in the colleges contribute to the status passage to adulthood, helped by the extended age range involved, 16-25 and beyond. Young people report very positively that they are 'treated as adults'. In allowing and encouraging young people to exercise a reasonable degree of responsibility and self-determination, the evidence suggests that the colleges are significantly contributing to the process of becoming adult citizens, if failing to provide broad perspectives via the content of the curriculum (Rudd and Evans, 1998).

Among German young adults, research findings have indicated a wider interest and involvement in activities associated with citizenship than is apparent in their English counterparts. Samples were divided into four groups identified with broad occupational routes: academic/professional, skilled, semi-skilled, unskilled. As might be expected, in both countries interest in politics and in the intention to vote declined from the academic and professionally oriented groups to the unskilled group. Less expected was the finding that, in every group, substantially more German young people than English exhibited these elements of citizenship. Even among those on the academic career track, the young Germans were 20 per cent ahead. Self-efficacy and self-confidence in skills and abilities were also significantly higher in the German sample, as was work commitment, as the figures in Chapter 3 showed.

The German approach typifies that of many European countries. Green (1995) has observed 'the tendency in many European countries to resist any approaches which reduce theoretical and general educational components of VET, since these are essential not only for skills transfer but also for the

---

[1] Initial findings from extended Anglo-German study (1997-1998) focusing on transitions in labour markets of the Eastern part of Germany, carried out by Karen Evans, Jens Kaluza and Martina Behrens .

potential of individuals both as citizens and as learners and employees seeking to progress to higher levels' (p 25). Narrow versions of the competence-based curriculum may contribute to the process of becoming economically independent in an individualistic sense. They are however contradictory to processes of maximal development of citizenship since they neither equip with critical skills nor cultivate the sense of shared autonomy in the broader context within which individual 'biographical projects' are pursued. They may also reinforce and reflect structural inequalities which deny citizenship in its full sense to increasing numbers of marginalised people.

Beyond Dualisms

In the 'risk society' success is seen as increasingly dependent on individual skill and capability as well as external risks and ability to judge and manipulate them. 'Navigation' may involve 'shooting the rapids' or being overtaken by a tide of events which have been set in train. In Giddens' words' it feels like a world spinning out of control, felt in individual lives.' The world of uncertainty is not a result of the limits of knowledge but its runaway character is tied up with the progression of knowledge itself - it is 'manufactured uncertainty'. Founders of the enlightenment linked to the role of science the simple and attractive idea that the more we know about ourselves and the world, the more we will be able to master it. In our late 20th Century experience the progression of knowledge does not create the rational control envisaged; rather, it creates experiences of new uncertainties and new risks, an open future which has to be navigated.

Are we responding to this by simply replacing the submissive man produced by factory processes of schooling with the flexible conforming person of government schemes and new vocational qualifications, equipped with limited competences and a few 'transferable' skills?

This raises another set of issues about the changing interfaces between education and work, with the transfer of knowledge, skill and experience between educational and work settings of central significance. A range of 'dualisms' limits our approaches to questions of learning and its vocational effects (Marginson, 1994). Dualism is represented, for example, in the distinctions between the 'vocational and relevant' and the 'academic and liberal' traditions in education. It is also represented in the opposing approaches to 'structure and agency' which argue that individuals determine their own fates and those which argue that agents are subject to, and determined by, external forces. Questions of 'choice or determination' are strongly represented in discussions of career pathways. As Chapter 4 has shown, much early literature on occupational choice saw individuals as context-free agents; Roberts et al (1968) took the opposite view, arguing that there was little choice involved. Careers were determined by social structures and individuals were launched on trajectories with the flight path and end point more or less fixed.

The polarised perspectives that set *"people make society"* against *"society makes people"* have been displaced by approaches which recognise that the field of human actions is structured and that these structures can themselves be negotiated and changed by those who operate within them. If we accept this premise we are no longer locked into waiting for the social policies and the broad social structures within which we operate to change fundamentally before educational practice based on alternative values becomes possible.

The arguments which move beyond dualism are about the dynamics of transformation, the 'dialogical relationships' of Giddens (1991). Institutions are continuously created and re-created by the individuals who live and work within them. When these ideas are applied to the relationship between education and work, a new conception of 'work-related' education become possible. The challenge in establishing new relationships between education and work is to reduce the gap that separates them without impinging on the unique features of each. Work can be made more educative and education more relevant to work without dissolving one into the other. Further changes need to be made to the world of work and the structures of work and the labour market as well as to education if the new relationships between education and work are to be well founded (Evans and Brown, 1991). Moreover, education has a plurality of purposes. As Marginson contends, it is no more tenable to argue, for example, that a University should be subordinated to the economy, that is Government and industry, than it is to claim total self-regarding autonomy for the community of scholars.

Some argue that by broadening vocational education, redefining it to incorporate some aspect of 'liberal' education, it becomes preparation for life. This is one way in which instrumental orientations of the work-related curriculum are brought into the wider domains of education for adult life and citizenship. But can the multiple purposes of education be resolved in a simple 'broadening' of work-related studies in this way? The same analysis could be applied to further education in the 1990s, where generic skills and key skills are emphasised and seen as central to this process of 'broadening' work-related education. They are represented as being in the general interest of society yet they are derived from and defined in terms of the needs of employers. Generic skills are sometimes presented as being superior to knowledge since the skills, being context free, are timeless and independent while knowledge is seen as provisional and context bound. Whether context-free transferability is possible in the way suggested by the proponents of 'key skills' is debatable, since the 'freeing' of skills from their contexts can lead to superficiality and detaches 'flexibility' from deeper capability (Barnett, 1994). As propounded, key skills reflect a restricted set of social values, derived from the needs of employers. Education, as distinct from training, must maintain a degree of independence from any particular dominant set of social values. For this, critical skills and research-mindedness have to be preserved alongside the development of capabilities and competence. In approaches based on experiential learning, education is distinct from the experience it draws upon. Work and community experience are coupled with critical reflection, conceptualisation, knowledge and action, in an iterative process of learning (Chisnall, 1983). Multiple purposes are embodied within the learning without collapsing it into the work and community experience which it seeks to use as one resource, among many others.

Education for uncertainty

Much time, energy and resource has been expended in grappling with the dualisms of the historic academic/vocational divide in post-16 education. How can new relationships between education and work, dimly perceived and only just being forged, feed into the generation of new structures? The saying that 'life is best understood backwards but has to be lived forwards' can usefully be adapted here. Post-16 education in Britain has suffered from an approach which adds bits and endlessly re-organises, the Dearing Report recommendations being the latest example of this. Surely it is better to think of the ultimate goal, the Learning Society, and work backwards from there? The triple track approach of previous government policy encourages divided and divisive wastes and inordinate amounts of time in sterile debates about parity of esteem. If the aim is real flexibility and mobility, defined in learner (rather than employer) terms, that has to be built in structurally. A climbing frame structure is required, with recognised ways up and across which can be followed, accompanied by full credit transfer and accumulation. In the climbing frame the ways up will have to meet criteria of breadth and coherence as well as depth in a chosen specialism. Scotland has chosen a form of climbing frame. But Scotland is, apparently, too different socially and culturally for the lessons to be taken; this said while looking eastwards to Germany, Japan and even Singapore! (Dearing Interim Report 1995).

Why a climbing frame structure? First, it is more likely to maximise achievement, by removing barriers and inflexibilities of the triple track of academic, applied and work-based studies. Second, it is more likely to meet national targets. Third, parity of esteem, that great time waster, becomes a non-issue. Learners climb as far and as fast as they are able and wish at any time, with the opportunity to carry forward credit, return and resume studies at any time, at any age. This is not incompatible with what the Dearing Report has done, because it is relatively easy to see how, with the political will, the Dearing 16-19 reforms provide the first step towards this. What other criteria need to be applied?

Changing the culture of education and training

- *Establish broad-based education and training after 16 as the 'norm' with the aim of improving achievement to world class standards of breadth and depth.*
- *Climbing frame structure, encouraging an enlarged curriculum with flexible combinations of general, vocational and work-based elements, not age-tied.*
- *Restrict the youth labour market, one of the 'pull' factors: make it difficult to employ young people under 18 full-time without providing quality training opportunities either individually or in partnership.*
- *Allow a work-based route to qualification, using employers able, individually or in groups, to provide quality careerships and apprenticeships.*
- *Emphasise entitlements to learning as well as outcomes.*
- *Invest in the training culture: train trainers and key workers (in response to evidence that many of the problems are internal to industry itself).*

The argument about the need to establish breadth *and* depth is effectively won, and the initial down-playing of the need for broader knowledge as well as specific competence in vocational qualifications is now recognised as a huge policy error. The Dearing Report can be seen as a first step towards the climbing frame approach. Turning to the third point, the restriction of the youth labour market is not popular because it requires reforms on the other side of the equation, in labour market and employment practices, but the evidence shows it to be necessary. Allowing a work-based route to qualification recognises its importance as a route but requires better incentives and support for provision of educational breadth, as well as giving priority to training trainers and key workers, in response to evidence that many of the problems are internal to industry itself. Finally, of course, targeted financial support must be provided to enable people to participate, and withstand the difficulties of study. These issues have their mirror image in Germany where the challenge now is to improve and re-orientate the Berufsschule with more flexible partnerships between educational institutions and industry which enable the former to provide those elements of education and training which the latter are now finding increasingly difficult to sustain.

The need for 'future-oriented' education

But there is a dimension missing from all this: future oriented education has to transform, not reproduce. What do we have to do to live in this world of manufactured uncertainty? We must constantly use information to engage with the world and we have to deal with the flood of information and views with which we are daily bombarded. In particular, more critical engagement with science and technology is needed, recognising that the runaway nature of technology is much more significant than anything political leaders might do. Moreover, there is a quest for a sense of self and for a new sense of what citizenship means in a world which feels increasingly out of our control. Some of these phenomena are reflected in calls for reworking of a moral framework for society. Intergenerational transmission turned on its head, young adults in our colleges and universities and places of work know more about living in the risk society than those who teach and supervise them. The challenge for those who teach and support them is to remain confident in an age of perceived risk and uncertainty, not to pretend that we are teaching them to cope in this new order of things.

If education is to be transformative, not reproductive, the role of education at all levels is to develop educated attributes. These incorporate core skills, key skills and transferable skills in their various manifestations, but go far beyond these. Core skills may enable us to survive, to stay afloat in the rapids. They do not encourage us to think about the influences we have on our context, individually and collectively, and we have been in danger of raising a new generation engaged in ego-driven projects with no sense of mutual responsibility: Thatcher's children, perhaps, to whom there is no such thing as society. The Speaker's Commission on Citizenship in 1990 concluded that the skills of citizenship need to be learned and the greatest challenge for the future is to create a society in which all can actively participate, can understand, can influence, can campaign and whistle-blow and work together in pursuit of the common good. What are the real educated attributes needed for the new forms of 'active citizenship'? They are the critical skills and dispositions that go hand in hand with the knowledge society, the information society. They need to be cultivated at all levels, with Higher Education there to secure and promote the highest forms of learning with understanding, critical skills, creativity and, above all, lifelong learning and inquiry centre stage. Knowing how is *not* the same as knowing why, and the social dynamics of the time demand that we know 'why' as well as 'how'.

To develop maximal versions of citizenship does require at the very least an enlargement of the curriculum. Silver and Brennan (1988) have argued that the enlarged curriculum should feature:

- Studies selected from several disciplines;
- Problem-solving related to real world problems;
- Breadth of courses and of outcomes;
- Concern with long-term employment needs;
- Concern to produce questioning and critical adults;
- An openness to external influences.

Developing competence into capability and linking this with the exercise of citizenship in maximal terms means bringing together some of the more successful learner-centred teaching and learning processes developed in English Further Education, coupled with the breadth of curriculum found in other parts of Europe. The effective worker has also to be an educated citizen. Maximal versions of citizenship are framed by cultural discourses as well as moral, political and egalitarian discourses identified by Arnot (1996). Meanings and understandings are culturally situated. This means that humanities education also plays a continuing role in what the learner needs to know. But achievement of maximal versions of citizenship requires more than this. It requires approaches to teaching and learning which promote shared autonomy in decision-making and arriving at judgements. There is also a need to move beyond enlargement of the curriculum to make it more effectively inclusive of diversity and difference in operational terms. This includes fostering dispositions of learners to challenge and to 'speak out', as well as to seek peaceful resolutions of conflict and differences (White 1996, Rowe 1997).

Support services are required which encourage proactive rather than passive transition behaviours. These have to be made available in ways which are less dependent on the cultural capital of users. Market based approaches are inappropriate in this context. Much of the market-based drive to 'empower' young people take more control over their own learning and make 'better' life and career decisions has been based on two misunderstandings. Firstly, markets which fund providers for recruitment and achievement actually reduce the chances of most young people exerting control over their own learning (Hodkinson and Sparkes, 1994). Vouchers such as Youth Credits cannot redress the power imbalance between employers and training providers on the one hand and young people on the other. Institutions funded through such market imbalances cannot afford to allow young people to choose something which is not in the institution's own interests. Secondly, there is evidence that young people change during the process of post-school education and training. These changes in self-perception, attitude and identity mean that it is impossible to make a decision at 16+ that 'correctly' identifies a future career which is inevitably largely unknown. Learning implies change in the learner, and programmes are needed which facilitate and support personal growth rather than penalising providers and learners when a significant change occurs. Balancing specialism with much greater breadth and flexibility ensures that young people can open out their horizons, rather than narrow them down (Evans et al, 1997).

Changes in practice in guidance include learner-centred initiatives in which young people assess their own achievements and capabilities and negotiate development plans drawing on resources from inside and outside the school or college. 'Compacts', whereby employers, training providers and young people work together in setting achievable personal goals, have been successful in encouraging those who worked hard but achieved only modest examination results. On a broader front, such approaches are undermined when young people's aspirations were already at a very low level, often as a direct result of the lack of opportunity and experience of repeated failure. Where labour market conditions place considerable restrictions on the pathways open, more individualised, learner-centred guidance may become necessary. But under-resourced services are unable to deliver such support effectively, because of the sheer size of case loads (Bimrose and Brown, 1991).

A 'redistributive' approach to social and financial support provides targeted support to optimise individual and group life chances to negotiate transition structures successfully.

As Chapter 6 showed, when person-centred approaches are used to produce attitude change, empowerment and participation, they must be *combined* with measures which alter the material and social environment, to remedy situations which have placed such great demands that many young people cannot cope unaided. If the contract between young people and society has broken down, as writers as geographically distant as Coffield (in

Teeside) and Dwyer (in Melbourne, Australia) conclude, this must be restored before any more demands can be made for young people to take greater responsibility for themselves.

Education, housing and employment are the bases for establishing independent adult status, and society must provide as necessary conditions for successful transition
- Targeted help and guidance from specialist agencies, without penalties for 'wrong' decisions
- Financial support to complete or continue education and training
- Access to affordable housing.
- Minimum wage to meet basic living costs, if employed
- Support for training and living costs if unemployed and without parental support.

These measures are necessary to break the vicious circles which operate for those who come from low income families and are at high risk of becoming victims of poverty themselves, going through adult life as 'permanent transients' (Dwyer, 1991) unable to participate as citizens in any meaningful way. These are not, however, measures for just 'the disadvantaged', but for all who experience the effects of increased risk, blocked opportunities and an increasingly hostile labour market.

They are necessary, but not sufficient, conditions for active engagement and participation. Understanding of the self in relation to others is also essential if real personal 'agency' is to develop. This requires the recognition that the self can only find its meaning and value in membership of communities, whether these be local communities, communities of shared interest or communities of practice. Active forms of individualisation, emphasising action competences and dispositions of the individual, must be accompanied by reconnection into communities. The influence of the education professional, whether teacher, youth worker or counsellor, lies in stimulating fresh perspectives on capabilities, possibilities and relationships. Thus the goal of all programmes must be to promote:
- Self esteem and identity formation
- Basic skills and abilities to cope effectively with demands of the environment, in the community and workplace
- Understanding of diversity, difference and the relationship of self to others
- The dispositions and skills necessary for participation in 'communicative action', particularly with peers.

Bringing the elements together

The four shifts from enlargement to inclusion, from core skills to educated attributes, from reproduction to redistribution and from passive to active individualisation are mutually reinforcing:

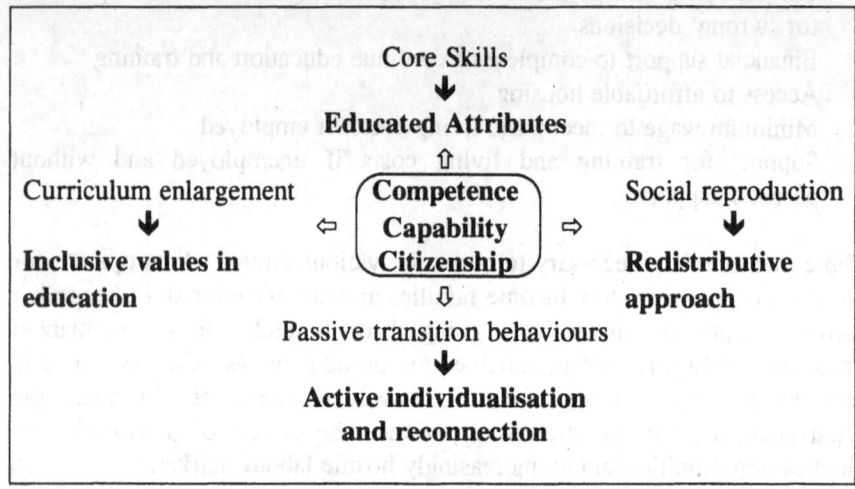

Figure 7.1: Education for citizenship

They create the possibility for progress towards maximal versions of citizenship, incorporating competence and capability for action and social contribution. If key skills can be embedded in and permeate the curriculum for all people in all contexts, so can the values and goals advanced above, with the political will.

In the move from enlargement to inclusion, and from key skills to educated attributes, the workplace cannot be the 'ultimate curriculum authority' and neither can the 'academy'.

The curriculum must relate, at any age or stage, to a framework for interpreting the world as a 'social whole', to use Sedunary's (1996) expression, while understanding the sources of diversity and differentiation within it. In conjunction with this, inclusive policies, strategies and forms of educational support are needed which value and recognise the capabilities of all, policies which recognise diversity and move away from assumptions about the condition of the age group as a whole. The idea that a curriculum based on bundles of core and vocational skills combined with action planning will equip young people for the future is wholly inadequate.

Policies need to be based on more holistic analyses of social dynamics and an understanding of ways in which experiences in early adulthood can give stability or instability to the life course. This transcends national, or even European boundaries, as earlier studies have demonstrated (Evans and Haffenden, 1991). Effective education for the future depends on the extent of free and equal access and the 'redistributive' mechanisms for resources and social support which are employed; the ways in which provision is linked structurally and methodologically, and relates to the life course; the ways in which education links and draws upon different domains of experience in work, community and family. Moreover, future oriented, maximal versions of education for citizenship derive their values from what is required for the ethical advancement of society and the state, and it is these, above and beyond the values of the workplace and the immediate requirement for material economic progress, which shape effective learning for citizenship at all levels.

Being useful and being virtuous are important - but the overriding aim of education must be to produce a society consisting as far as possible of persons who have independence of mind and who are morally free. The health and long-term preservation of the democratic state is dependent on its members. Lifelong and comprehensive educational opportunity made equally available and accessible to all is ultimately to its advantage. Only education which develops citizenship and competence in their maximal senses, and promotes favourable conditions for their practice, will ensure empowered and participatory communities able both to support the successful pursuit of individual projects and to play their part in the social and political processes which will shape the socio-economic scenarios of the future.

Bibliography

Ainley, P. (1994), *Class and Skill*, Cassell, London and New York.
Alheit, P. (1995), The Biographical Question as a Challenge to Adult Education, *Scottish Journal of Adult and Continuing Education*, Vol.2, No.1, pp.75-91.
Anyon, J. (1983), Intersections of Gender and Class. Accommodation and Resistance by Working Class and Affluent Females to Contradictory Sex-Role Ideologies in Walker, S and Barton, L (eds.),*Gender, Class and Education*, Lewes, Falmer Press.
Arnot, M. (1997), Gendered Citizenry: new feminist perspectives on education and citizenship, *British Educational Research Journal*, Vol.23, No.3, June 1997, pp.275-296.
Ashton, D. and Field, D. (1976), Young Workers, Hutchinson, London.
Association of Teachers in Technical Institutions (1972), *The education of the 16 - 19 age group*, ATTI, London.
Atkinson, A. B., Ramwater, L., Smeeding, T.M. (1995), *Income Distribution in OECD Countries: Evidence from the Luxembourg Income Study*, OECD Social Policy Studies, Paris.
Ausubel, D. P. (1954), *Theories and Problems of Adolescent Development*. Grune and Stratton, New York.
Avis, J. (1993), A New Orthodoxy, Old Problems: post-sixteen reform *British Journal of Sociology of Education*, Vol.14, No.3, pp.245-260.
Baethge, M. (1989), Individualisation as hope or disaster in Hurrelmann K and Engel U (eds.), *The Social World of Adolescents*, de Gruyter, Berlin.
Banks, M., Bates, I., Breakwell, G., Bynner, J., Emler, N., Jameson, J. and Roberts, K. (1992), *Careers and Identities*, Open University Press, Buckingham.
Ball, C. (1991), *Learning Pays*, Royal Society of Arts, London.
Ball, S. (1990), *Politics and Policy Making in Education*, Routledge, London.

Barnett, R. (1994), The Limits of Competence, Society for Research in Higher Education, London.
Bates, I. (1993), 'A Job Which is 'Right for Me'?' in Bates, I. and Riseborough, G. (eds.), *Youth and Inequalities*, Buckingham, Open University Press.
Bates, I. and Riseborough, G. (eds.), (1993), *Youth and Inequality*, Buckingham, Open University Press.
Beaumont, G. (1995), *Review of 100 NVQs and SVQs:* A Report submitted to the Department of Education and Employment, London.
Beck, U. (1992), *Risk Society,* Sage Publications, London.
Bernstein, B. (1981), Codes, modalities and the process of cultural reproduction: a model, *Language and Society*, 10, pp.327-63.
Bimrose, J. and Brown, A. (1991), Inadequacy of learner-centred models of guidance in practice: interplay of policy, resources and implementation issues. Fourth EARLI Conference, Turku.
Blackman, S. and Evans, K. (1994), Comparative Skill Acquisition in Germany and England *Youth and Policy*, Issue No.43, pp.1-23.
Board of Education (1909), *Consultative Committee Report on Attendance Compulsory or otherwise, at Continuation Schools*, Cmnd 4758, HMSO, London.
Board of Education (1917), *Departmental Committee on Juvenile Education in relation to Employment after the War*, Final report, Cmnd 8512 'Lewis Report' HMSO, London.
Board of Education (1939a), *The Service of Youth* Circular 1486, 1, HMSO, London.
Board of Education (1939b), *The Challenge of Youth* Circular 1516, 1, HMSO, London.
Board of Education (1941), *The Registration of Youth* Circular 1577, HMSO, London.
Board of Education (1943), *The Youth Service after the War*, HMSO, London.
Bone, M. and Ross, E. (1972), *The Youth Service and Similar Provision for Young People*, 29, HMSO, London.
Borow, H. (1996), Development of occupational motives and roles in Hoffman, L.W. and Hoffman, M.L. (eds.) *Review of child Development Research*, 2, Russell Sage Foundation.
Bourdieu, P. (1990), Die biographische Illusion in Bois, Jg.3 Hft.1, pp.75-81.
Bowles, S. and Gintis, H. (1976), Schooling in Capitalist America, Routledge and Kegan Paul, London.

Brown, A. (1994), *Review of the characteristics of effective learning programmes for the development of occupational competence* Report to Department of Employment, University of Surrey, Guildford.

Brown, A. and Bimrose, J. (1993), Admissions to higher education, *Journal of Access Studies*, Vol.8, pp.154-158.

Brown, A., Evans, K., Blackman, S., Germon, S. (1994), *Key Workers: Technical and Training Mastery in the Workplace*, Hyde Publications, Bournemouth.

Brown, P. and Lauder, H. (1992), *Education for Economic Survival: from Fordism to Post-Fordism*, Routledge, London.

Brown, R. (1995), Unemployment, Youth and the Employment Relationship, *Education and Training for the Future Labour Markets of Europe Conference*, University of Durham, September 1995.

Bulmer, M. and Rees, A.M. (1996), *Citizenship Today*, UCL Press, London.

Bury, M.O. (1972), *The Industrial Training Act* Paper presented to Association of Colleges of Further and Higher Education (ACFHE), p.9.

Bynner, J. (1990), *Youth politics and lifestyle*, ESRC 16-19 Initiative Occasional Paper.

Bynner, J. (1994), *Changing Needs, New Structures? Lessons for Vocational Preparation*, CEDAR International Conference, University of Warwick, April 15.

Bynner, J. and Roberts, K. (eds.) (1991), *Youth and Work: Transitions and Employment in England and Germany*, Anglo-German Foundation, London.

Callaghan, J. (1976), Speech launching the 'Great Debate on Education', Ruskin College, Oxford, October 1976.

Carmichael, L. (1992), The competency movement: professional and vocational education in *Competency and Professional Education* Conference Proceedings, University of Canberra, Canberra, 55-68.

Chanan, G. (1976), To sustain life-schools' concepts of adult work, *New Universities Quarterly*, Winter, pp.37-46.

Chester, R.L.C. (1968), Youth, Education and work: A revised perspective, *Social and Economic Administration*, 2, pp.41-53.

Chisholm, L. and Bergeret, J-M. (1991), *Young People in the European Community: Towards an agenda for research and policy*. Brussels, EC Task Force Human Resources, Youth, Training and Education.

Chisnall, H. (1993), *Learning from Work and Community Experience*, NFER-Nelson, Slough.

City and Guilds of London Institute (1974), *Further Education of 16 - 19 year olds by part-time day release*. Memorandum to the Secretary of State for Education and Science, CGLI, London.

Cockram, L. and Beloff, H. (1978), *Rehearsing to be adults*. National Youth Bureau, Leicester, 3-4.

Coleman, J.C. (1986), The Focal Theory of Adolescence: A Psychological Perspective in Hurrelmann, K and Engel, U (eds.) *The Social World of Adolescents: International Perspectives*, Walter de Gruyter, Berlin, New York.

Coleman, J.S. (1961), *The Adolescent Society*, 3, Glencoe Free Press, New York.

Coleman, J.S. et al (1974), *Youth and Transition to Adulthood*. Report of the Panel on Youth of Presidents Science Advisory Committee, University of Chicago Press, Chicago.

Coles, R. (1996), Vulnerable Groups and Social Exclusion. Paper presented at the ESRC/ISA-Sponsored Conference - British Youth Research: A New Agenda, University of Glasgow, pp.26-28, January.

Dahrendorf, R. (1997), Citizenship and Social Class in *Citizenship Today*, Bulmer, M. and Rees, A.M. (eds.), UCL Press, London.

Dale, R. (1985), Education, Training and Employment: towards a new vocationalism?, Pergamon, Oxford.

Dalin, P. (1983), Towards learning by participation - an international perspective in Chisnall, H. (ed.) Learning from Work and Community Experience, NFER-Nelson, Slough.

Davies, B.D. and Gibson, A. (1967), *The Social Education of the Adolescent*, University of London Press Ltd, London.

Dearing, R. (1996), *Review of qualifications for 16-19 year olds*, HMSO, London.

Department of Education and Science (1964), Special Committee *Day Release*, HMSO, London.

Department of Education and Science (1969), *Youth and Community Work in the 70s*, 73, HMSO, London.

Department of Education and Science (1976), *Unified Vocational Preparation*, HMSO, London.

Department of Education and Science (1981), *Education for 16-19 year olds*, MacFarlane Report, HMSO, London.

Department of Education and Science (1982), Experience and Participation (Thompson Report), HMSO, London.

Department of Education and Science/Department of Employment (1979),
a) *16-18: Education and Training for 16-18 year olds*, HMSO, London.
b) *Providing Educational Opportunities for 16-18 year olds*, HMSO, London.
c) *A Better Start in Working Life*, HMSO, London.

Department of Education and Science/Department of Employment (1979), *A Better Start in Working Life*, 2, HMSO, London.

Department of Education and Science/ Department of Employment (1979), *16-18: Education and Training for 16-18 year olds*, 6, HMSO, London.
Department of Employment/Department of Education and Science (1991), *Education and Training for the 21st Century*, HMSO, London.
DES/DE (1990) From the decade of the Enterprise Culture to the decade. *Education and Training for the 21st Century*, HMSO, London.
Dewey, J. (1916, 1933), *Democracy and Education*, Free Press, New York.
Dwyer, P. and Wyn, J. (1994) Post-compulsory Pathways Through Education and Training: Metaphor or Reality? Rethinking Policies for Young People, Youth Research Centre, University of Melbourne
Education Act (1918), 8 and 9, Geo.5, Chap.21, Fisher.
Education Act (1944), 7 and 8, Geo.6, Chap.31, Butler.
Edwards, R. (1993), The Inevitable Future?: Post-Fordism in Work and Learning in Edwards, R., Sieminski, S., Zeldin, D. (eds.) *Adult Learners, Education and Training*, Routledge, London and New York.
Entwhistle, H. (1979), *Antonio Gramsci Conservative Schooling for Radical Politics*, Routledge and Kegan Paul, London.
Eraut, M. (1993), Assessment of Competence in higher level occupations: Implications for student development *Competence and Assessment 21*, pp.14-17.
Erikson, E.H. (1968), *Identify, Youth and Crisis*. Norton, New York.
Etzioni, A. (1995), *The Spirit of Community - Rights, Responsibilities and the Communitarian Agenda*, Fontana, London.
Evans, K. (1980), *Day Release*. Further Education Curriculum Review and Development Unit, London.
Evans, K. (1989), Post-16 Education and Training: Educational Provision and Outcomes in Two Contrasting Areas. *British Journal of Education and Work*, Vol.3, No.2, pp.44-59.
Evans K. (1994), *Leisure Patterns of Young Adults in Britain and the Role of the Youth Service*, International Journal of Adolescence and Youth, Vol.4, No.4, pp.179-195.
Evans, K. (1995), Competence and Citizenship: towards a complementary model for times of critical social change. *British Journal of Education and Work*, Vol.8, No.1, pp.14-27.
Evans, K. (1997), *The interplay between work and education among young adults in Canada and Britain*. Canadian Congress of Learned Societies, CASAE, St John's, Newfoundland.
Evans, K. Behrens, M. and Kaluza, J. (1998), *Socio-economic attitudes and beliefs of young adults in Eastern Germany: a comparison with Britain and West Germany, Project Report*, University of Surrey/Anglo-German Foundation, Guildford.

Evans, K. and Haffenden, I. (1991), *Education for Young Adults: International Perspectives*, Routledge, London.

Evans, K. and Heinz, W. (1994), *Becoming Adults in England and Germany*, Anglo-German Foundation, London and Bonn, Anglo-German Foundation.

Evans, K. and Hodkinson, P., Keep, E., Maguire, M., Rainbird, H., Senker, P., Raffe, D., Unwin, L. (1997), *Working to Learn*, Institute of Personnel and Development, London.

Evans, K. and Kaluza, J. (1997), Interim report on Trainers', Young Adults' Experiences in the Eastern Part of Germany, ZAROF, Leipzig.

Fearey, P.W. and Lalor, O. (1991), Youth and Higher Education in the USSR in Evans, K. and Haffenden, I. *Education for Young Adults*, Routledge, London.

Field, J. (1995), Reality Testing in the Workplace: are NVQs 'Employment-led'? in Hodkinson P and Issitt M (eds.) *The Challenge of Competence*, Cassell, London and New York.

Finch, J. (1995), Family responsibilities and rights, in Bulmer, M. (Ed) *Citizenship Today: the contemporary relevance of T H Marshall*, UCL Press, London.

Finegold, D. and Soskice, D. (1990), The Failure of Training in Britain: Analysis and Prescription, in Esland, G. (Ed) *Education, Training and Employment Vol.1: Educated Labour*, Addison-Wesley, Open University, Wokingham.

Francis, A. (1995), Improving the UK's industrial competitiveness: do we know how and would we know if we were succeeding? *Royal Society of Arts Journal*, October Issue, pp. 25-31.

Freire, P. (1972a), *Pedagogy of the Oppressed*, Penguin, Harmondsworth.

Freire, P. (1972b), *Cultural Action for Freedom*, Penguin, Harmondsworth.

Freire, P. (1974), *Education: The Practice of Freedom*, Writers and Readers, London.

Friedenberg, E.Z. (1959), *The Vanishing Adolescent*, Beacon Press, Boston.

Funnell, P. and Muller, D. (eds.), (1991), *Vocational Education and the challenge of Europe*, Kogan Page, London.

Furlong, A. and Biggart, A. (1995), 'Social Reproduction in an Urban Context: Neighbourhoods, Labour Markets and Discouraged Workers' British Sociological Association Annual Conference, Leicester.

Furlong, A. and Cartmel, F. (1997), *Young People and Social Change*, Open University Press, Buckingham.

Garner, C. Main, B. and Raffe, D. (1987), Local Variations in *School Leaver Employment and Unemployment within Large Cities*, University of Edinburgh, Centre for Educational Sociology.

Garner, C. and Raudenbausch, S.W. (1991), Neighbourhood Effects on Educational Attainment: A Multi-Level analysis, *Sociology of Education*, Vol.64, pp.251-262.
Giddens, A. (1991), *Modernity and Self-identity: Self and Society in the late modern age*, Polity Press, Cambridge.
Giddens, A. (1996), T.H. Marshall, The state and democracy in Bulmer, M. and Rees, A.M. (eds.) *Citizenship Today*, UCL Press, London.
Ginzberg, E. (1972), Toward a theory of occupational choice: A restatement. *Vocational Guidance Quarterly*, 290, pp.169-176.
Giroux, H. (1989), *Schooling and Democracy*, Routledge, London.
Gleeson, D. (ed.)(1990), *Training and its alternatives*, Open University Press, Buckingham.
Gorz, A. (1989), *Critique of Economic Reason*, Verso, London.
Gottfredson, L.S. (1981), Circumspection and Compromise: A Development Theory of Occupational Aspirations, *Journal of Counselling Psychology*, Vol.28, pp.545-579.
Gray, J., Jesson, D. and Sime, E. (1992), 'The Discouraged Worker Revisited: Post-16 Participation in Education South of the Border', *Sociology*, Vol.26, pp.493-505.
Green, A. (1995), *The European Challenge to British Vocational Education and Training* in Hodkinson, P. and Issitt, M. (eds.), The Challenge of Competence, Cassell, London and New York.
Griffin, C. (1985), *Typical Girls?*, Routledge, London.
Habermas, J. (1976), *Legitimation Crisis*, Heinemann, London.
Habermas, J. (1991), *The Theory of Communicative Action*, Polity Press, Cambridge.
Hall, S. and Jefferson, T. (eds.) (1976), *Resistance through Rituals*, Hutchinson, London.
Hamachek, D.E. (1976), in Adams, J.F. *Understanding Adolescence* (3rd Edition), Allyn and Bacon Inc.
Hargreaves, D. (1967), *Social Relations in Secondary School*, Routledge and Kegan Paul, London.
Harris, D.B. (1977), Work and the Adolescent Transition to Maturity in Cottle, T.J. (ed.) *Readings in Adolescent Psychology: Contemporary Perspectives*. Harper and Row, New York.
Havighurst, R.J. (1953), *Human Development and Education*. Longmans Green,
Heater, D. (1990), *Citizenship: the Civic Ideal in World History, Politics and Education*, Longman, London.
Herford, M.E.M. (1969), School to Work, in Caplan G and Lebovici S *Adolescence-Psychosocial Perspectives*. Basic Books, Inc, 156,

Hill, J.P. and Monks, F.J. (eds.),in *Adolescence and Youth in Prospect.* IPC Science and Technology Press, 53.

Hodkinson, P. and Sparkes, A.C. (1994), The Myth of the Market: The Negotiation of Training in a Youth Credits Pilot Scheme, *British Journal of Education and Work*, Vol. , No.3, pp.5-19.

Hurrelmann, K. (1988), *Social Structure and Personality Development*, Cambridge University Press, Cambridge.

Issitt, M. (1995), Competence, Professionalism and Equal Opportunities in *The Challenge of Competence* (ed.) Hodkinson, P. and Issitt, M., Cassell, London and New York.

Janne, H. (1974), The educational needs of the 16 - 19 age group *International Review of Education, 21*, pp. 127-148.

Jeffs, A.J. (1979), *Young People and the Youth Service*, Routledge and Kegan Paul, London.

Jenner, J. (1995), *Power, Participation or Control in Youth Work Practice*, MPhil thesis, University of Surrey.

Jones, G. and Wallace, C. (1992), *Youth, Family and Citizenship*, Open University Press, Buckingham.

Jones, L. and Moore, R. (1993), Education, Competence and the control of Expertise, *British Journal of Sociology of Education*, Vol.14, No.4, 1993, pp.385-397.

Jousselin, J. (1968), *The Organisation of Youth in Europe*, Council for Cultural Co-operation, 35, Council of Europe, Strasbourg.

JUSTICE (1997), *Poverty undermines rights in the UK*, Submission to United Nations Committee on Human Rights.

Kerschensteiner, G. (1911), *German Youth and Education for Citizenship*, 5th Edition, Villaret.

King, E.J. (1975), *Post-Compulsory Education: The Way Ahead*, Sage, London.

Kohlberg, L. and Gilligan, C. (1971), *Twelve to Sixteen*: Early Adolescence, Daedalus,

Krugman, P. (1994), *Competitiveness: A dangerous obsession*, Foreign Affairs, Vol.73, pp.28-45.

Labour Party, (1972), *Labour's Programme for Britain* Labour Party, London.

Lave, J. and Weiger, E. (1991), *Situated Learning : Legitimate Peripheral Participation*, Cambridge University Press, New York.

Lister, R. (1990), *The Exclusive Society: Citizenship and the Poor*, Child Poverty Action Group, London.

Lupton, T. (1963), *On the shop Floor, Two Studies of Workshop Organisation and Output*, Pergamon, Oxford.

Mac-an-Ghaill, M. (1996), State, Schooling and Social Class: beyond critiques of the 'new right' hegemony. *British Journal of Sociology of Education*, Vol.17, No.2, pp.163-176.

MacDonald, R. and Coffield, F. (1991), *Risky Business?* Falmer Press, Basingstoke.

McCulloch, G. (1995), *From education to work: the case of Technical Schools* in Bush, L. and Green, A., Youth, Education and Work, Kogan Page, Philadelphia/London.

McLaughlin, T.H. (1992), Citizenship, Diversity and Education: a Philosophical Perspective *Journal of Moral Education*, Vol.21, No.3, pp.239-250.

Manpower Services Commission (1982), *Youth Task Group Report*, MSC, Sheffield.

Marcus, I.M. (1969), 'From School to Work: Certain Aspects of Psychosocial Interaction' in Caplan G and Lebovici S (eds.) *Adolescence-Psychosocial Perspectives*. Basic Books Inc, 157,

Marginson, S. (1994), *The transferability of educated attributes*. Centre for the Study of Higher Education, University of Melbourne, Melbourne.

Marshall, T.H. (1952), *Citizenship and Social Class*, Cambridge University Press, Cambridge.

Mead, L.M. (1986), *Beyond Entitlement: the social obligations of citizenship*, Free Press, New York.

Miller, D. (1969), *The Age Between: Adolescents in a disturbed society*. Cornmarket, Hutchinson, London.

Ministry of Education (1945), *Youth's Opportunity: Further Education in County Colleges* Pamphlet No.3, HMSO, London.

Ministry of Education (1947), *Further Education: the scope and contents of its opportunities under the Education Act*, Pamphlet No 8, HMSO, London.

Ministry of Education (1959), Central Advisory Council for Education (England) *15 - 18 Crowther Report*, HMSO, London.

Ministry of Education (1959), *15-18: The Report of the Central Advisory Council for Education (England)* Crowther Report, HMSO, London.

Ministry of Education (1960), *The Youth Service in England and Wales*, Cmnd 929, HMSO, London.

Ministry of Education (1961), *Better Opportunities in Technical Education*, Cmnd 1254, HMSO, London.

Ministry of Labour (1962), *Industrial Training: Government Proposals*, Cmnd 1892, Para. 6, HMSO.

Moore, R. (1987), Education and the Ideology of Production *British Journal of Sociology of Education*, Vol.18, No.2, pp.227-242.

Morrell, F. (1991), The Work of the Speaker's Commission and its Definition of Citizenship in Fogelman, K. *Citizenship in Schools*, David Fulton, London.

National Association of Teachers in Further and Higher Education (1974), *Statement on a Curriculum for Extension of Day Release*, NATFHE, London.

National Commission on Education (1993), *Learning to Succeed*, Paul Hamlyn, London.

National Curriculum Council (1990), Curriculum Guidance 9, NCC, York.

National Youth Bureau (1990), *Danger or Opportunity*, NYB, Leicester.

Norman, R. (1992), Citizenship, Politics and Autonomy in Milligan, D. and Muler, W. W. (eds.) *Liberalism, Citizenship and Autonomy*, Avebury Press, Aldershot.

Norris, N. (1991), *The Trouble with Competence*, Cambridge Journal of Education 21 (3), pp. 331-334.

OECD *Education at a Glance: OECD Indicators*, Centre for Education Research and Innovation; OECD Education Statistics, 1985-92, OECD, Paris.

Oliver, D. and Heater, D. (1994), *The Foundations of Citizenship*, Harvester Wheatsheaf, Hertfordshire.

Pallas, A.M. (1993), Schooling in the course of Human Lives: The Social context of Education and Transition to Adulthood in Industrial Society *Review of Educational Research*, Winter 1993, Vol.63, No.4, pp.409-447.

Park, A. (1996), Teenagers and their politics in Jowell, R., Curtice, J., Park, A., Brook, L. and Ahrendt, D.(eds.) *British Social Attitudes Survey*, 12th Report, Dartmouth, Aldershot.

Paterson, L. and Raffe, D. (1995), Staying on in Full-time Education in Scotland: 1985-1991, *Oxford Review of Education*, Vol.21, pp3-23.

Piaget, J. (1972), 'Intellectual Evolution from Adolescence to Adulthood', *Human Development*, 15, pp.1-12.

President of the Board of Education (1943), *Educational Reconstruction*, Cmnd 6458, HMSO, London.

Pring, R. (1991), The Curriculum and the New Vocationalism, in Esland, G. (ed.) *Education, Training and Employment Vol.2: The Educational Response*, Addison-Wesley, Open University, Wokingham.

Pye, D. and Mac-an-Ghaill, M. (1996), Inherent Contradiction and the Search for an Answer: young people in the new vocational context. *International Sociology of Education Conference*, 5 January, University of Sheffield, Sheffield.

Quicke, J. (1992), Individualism and Citizenship: some problems and possibilities *International Studies in Sociology of Education*, Vol.2 (2), pp.147-164.
Raffe, D. (1991), Beyond the Mixed Model in Crouch, C. and Heath, A. (eds.) *Social Research and Social Reform*, pp.287-314, Oxford University Press, Oxford.
Raffe, D. and Willms, J.D. (1989), Schooling the Discouraged Worker: Local Labour market Effects on Educational Participation, *Sociology*, Vol.23, pp.559-581.
Ranson, S. (1994), *Towards the learning society*, Cassell, London.
Richardson, A. (1990), Talking about Commitment, The Princes Trust, London.
Roberts, K. (1968), The Entry into Employment : An approach towards a generational theory. *Sociological Review 16*, 2, pp.165-184.
Roberts, K. (1995), *Youth and Employment in Modern Britain*, Oxford University Press, Oxford.
Rowe, D. (1998), Value, Pluralism, Democracy and Education for Citizenship in Modgil, C. and Leicester, M. *Values, Education and Cultural Diversity*, Cassell, London.
Rudd, P. (1996), *Structure and Agency in Youth Transitions*, PhD thesis, University of Surrey.
Rudd, P. and Evans, K. (1998), Structure and Agency in Youth Transitions: Student Perspectives on Vocational Further Education, *Journal of Youth and Policy*, Vol.1, No.1, pp.39-62.
Sedunary, E. (1996), Neither new nor alien to progressive thinking: interpreting the convergence of radical education and the new vocationalism, in *Australia Journal of Curriculum Studies*, Vol.28, No.4, pp.369-396.
Senker, P. (1995), The development and implementation of National Vocational Qualifications: an engineering case study, *New Technology, Work and Employment Journal*,
Sewell, W.H. and Haller, A.O. (1967), 'Occupational Choices of Wisconsin Farm Boys', *Rural Sociology*, Vol.32, pp.37-55.
Sewell, W.H. and Hauser, R.M. (1993), *A Review of the Wisconsin Longitudinal Study of Social and Psychological Factors in Aspirations and Achievements: 1963-1993*. University of Wisconsin-Madison: Centre for Demography and Ecology.
Silver, H. and Brennan, J. (1988), *A Liberal Vocationalism*, Methuen, London.
Simons, D. (1966), *George Kerschensteiner*, Methuen, London.
Skilbeck, M., Tait, K., Lowe, M. (1986), *A Question of Quality*, Institute of Education, University of London.

Smith, G. (1982), *Democracy in Western Germany* (Second Edition) Heinemann Educational Books, London.
Smith, M. (1988), *Developing Youth Work*, Open University Press, Buckingham.
Smith, M. (1992), The Possibilities of Public Life: Educating in the Community, in *Education and Community: The Politics of Practice*, Allen, G. and Martin, I. (eds.), Cassell, London.
Smith, M. (1994), *Local Education: community, conversation, praxis,*: Open University Press, Buckingham.
Smithers, A. (1993), *All our Futures*, London Channel 4 Television, Dispatches, London.
Speakers Commission (1990), *Encouraging Citizenship*, HMSO, London.
Stierlin, H. and Ravenscroft, K. (1972), 'Varieties of Adolescent Separation Conflicts', *British Journal of Medical Psychology*, 45, pp.299-313.
Stradling, R. (1983), *Political Education in West Germany and Britain*, Hansard Society, London.
Storrie, T. (1992), 'Citizenship: a key concept', *International Journal of Community Education*, 1:2, pp.2-3.
Super, D.E. and Sverko, B. (eds.)(1995), Life Roles, Values and Careers, Josey-Bass Publishers, San Francisco.
Times Higher Education Supplement, (1997), *Citizenship is not just cricket, teachers warn*, THES, 31 January.
Venables, E. (1975), *The Local Tech: an agent of social mobility?* In Learning and Earning: Aspects of Day Release in Further Education, 14, NFER, Slough.
Walby, S. (1986), *Patriarchy at Work*, Polity, Cambridge.
Wall, W.D. (1948), *The Adolescent Child.* 7-8, Methuen & Co. Ltd, London.
Wall, W.D. (1968), *Adolescents In School and Society.* NFER, Slough.
Wall, W.D. (1975), *Constructive Education for Children*, Harrap, London.
Watts, A. (1983), *Education, Unemployment and the Future of Work*, Open University Press, Buckingham.
Weatherill, B. (1990), (Speaker's Commission) *Encouraging Citizenship*, HMSO, London.
Weeks, J. (1990), The value of difference in Rutherford, J. (ed.) *Identity: Community, Culture Difference*, Lawrence and Wishart, London.
Wellington, J. (1987), *Skills for the Future*, University of Sheffield, Sheffield.
White, P. (1996), *Civic Virtues and Public Schooling: Educating Citizens for a Democratic Society*, Teachers College Press (Advances in Contemporary Educational Thought, Vol.17), New York and London.

Whitty, G., Aggleton, P. and Rowe, G. (1996), Competing Conceptions of Quality in Social Education: Learning from the Experience of Cross-Curricular Themes in *Teaching and Learning in Changing Times*, ed. Hughes M, Blackwell, London.

Williamson, H. (1996), Youth Work and Citizenship. Paper presented at the British Youth Research Conference: a new agenda, University of Glasgow.

Windmiller, M. (1976), 'Moral Development in Adams, J.F. *Understanding Adolescence*, Allyn and Bacon Inc., pp.176-198.

Wyn, J. (1996), *Youth and Citizenship*, Melbourne Studies in Education, University of Melbourne.

Youth Service Development Council (1969), *Youth and Community Work in the 70s*, HMSO, London.